"God is within her,
she will not fail."
Psalm 46:5

BECOMING
A FIVEFOLD
MADAM

God is going to use His word to transform you into a
woman of divine power who reflects His beauty, becoming
five times as great of a woman as you were before.

LASHONE STRICKLAND

Tymm Publishing LLC
Columbia, SC

Paperback ISBN: 979-8-9914825-0-9
E-book ISBN: 979-8-9914825-1-6

Published by Tymm Publishing LLC
Columbia, SC 29201

Book Cover Design: TywebbinCreations.com
Editor: Darcy Werkman

CONTENTS

I give all honor to my Lord and Savior Jesus Christ. He is the Lord of my life, who makes all things possible for me. Thank you, Lord, for giving me life. Thank you for the ability and gift of writing (see Mathew 19:26). My heart and soul love you eternally. True, pure, and unconditional love and kindness come from you. I am so thankful for this everlasting fountain of love within you, my Heavenly Father.

I, Lashone Strickland, was inspired and led by God to write this book on behalf of women all over the world. Some of you might need guidance in discovering who you are, while some may need a breath of fresh air to restart, which could just be a different look or aspect in life. It could also be that you want to change but you're not sure where to start. Whatever your reason is, I'm here for you. My mission is to help you to become all that God sees you as, helping you to discover the madam inside of you. You need to grow into the picture God is painting of you and see yourself the way He does, totally walking in freedom. This is your birthright by the blood of Jesus. It is your life. You have the power to choose what you want and desire to be.

My prayer is to encourage you to live a healthy lifestyle and that God's anointing will follow and transform you as you read. Be transformed through the renewing of your mind, walking, talking, and thinking like a fivefold madam of the Lord (see Romans 12: 1-2).

DEDICATION

I would like to dedicate this book to my grandparents, the late Carrie and Waddy Miller Sr. They are both endearing to me. The love they gave me was unmeasurable. Prosperity and God's covenant blessings are the gifts that were spoken and demonstrated over me as a child. I will forever love and cherish you, Mama and Daddy.

Read Psalm 23. I was raised from this very scripture. If I didn't know anything else, I would know this.

THE PURPOSE

The purpose and existence of this book is to encourage, inspire, and help women become a fivefold madam. This means that you will invite Jesus into your heart, accepting Him as your Lord and Savior and confessing that He is Lord. You will study the word and principles of God. You will have an overflow of his anointing and presence in your life. You will remain in Christ through life's challenges, highs, and lows, keeping faith in all circumstances. God's strong hand is in your life, molding you and making you the best version of yourself. God is a redeemer.

"If you declare with your mouth, 'Jesus is Lord,' and believe in your heart that God raised him from the dead, you will be saved. For it is with your heart that you believe and are justified, and it is with your mouth that you profess your faith and are saved" (Romans 10:9-10).

ACKNOWLEDGEMENTS

My husband of twenty-six years, Garnell Strickland Jr. You have always loved, cherished, and supported me. Thank you for your unconditional love. You are a God-given life partner. This 1990's love is a rare one. You are my friend, rock, and companion. I love you endlessly without limits. My real-life Superman. Baby Boo 96 . . . if you know you know.

My children: Justin, Elijah, and Caleb. You are God's most precious gifts to me. You are my blessing that I will always fight for. I believe in you three. You are a triple blessing from the Lord. I will love you intentionally and eternally.

My grandchildren, whom I adore. I am crowned with many blessings to have you three and to watch you grow and help shape you into great children. Jailyn, Gigi, Za'mir, I love you always.

My mom, Carolyn Young. She is the first woman that I ever loved. Thank you for loving me. Thank you for never giving up on our relationship. Your dedication to your family is truly amazing. You have a heart of gold. You give to all of us so freely. I love you dearly.

My sister, Bonita Irby. God accomplished so much when he blessed me with you. You are loyal and true to me in so many ways. You are my prayer partner and best friend, and you will always have a special place in my heart. I love you without a doubt. Thank you for being the very best big sister anyone could ever be.

My beloved nephew and nieces: Daquan, Daja, and Angel. I'm so proud of you all. I love you all like there is no tomorrow. You will always have a home within me.

My father, the late David Hagood. I miss and love him so much. He gave me his most beloved treasure, his beautiful daughters. He loved us all. We all have a part of him. He lives on through us. Daddy was blessed with five baby girls. I love my sisters, and they will forever be one together. My sisters from oldest to youngest: Bonita, LaTasha, LaTonya, Lashone(me),

LaTrice. We had six boys and seven girls among us sisters.

My bonus nieces and nephews: Shundraus, Tori, Markyla, Jasmine, Sierra, and Brianna. I love y'all.

Aunt Angie. She has been like a second mom to me. From the time I got engaged at nineteen, she has been there for me. She always taught me right. She trained me in home decor as well as doing what's right. She always held my hand just when I needed her. She has been an angel to me. Uncle Charlie has always loved me. I love you both.

I want to thank Pastor Linda and Pastor Harold Anderson. They have been the best spiritual teachers in my life. I have received so many spiritual gifts that were given under their ministry. They have always been a cover for my family. I love you both.

Thank you, Prophetess Sallie and Pastor Eugene Parker. You have been amazing marriage counselors for my husband and I. Being a part of your marriage ministry and couples' retreats has grown and shaped our marriage, helping build a solid foundation in our marriage for a lifetime. Thank you for all your support and prayers for our family. I love you both.

Thank you to *Jewels For Grace,* Bonita, Lashone(me), Daetanya, Dawn, Ashley, Carolyn, Angie, Reschelle, Lisa, and Mary. These nine women have truly been a new birth in me. There is so much strength and power among us all. Thank you for the vision, Bonita. Thank you for sharing my thoughts and vision as well. We are Sister Jewels. We are all made differently, but we are all beautiful in His crown, fitting perfectly how He has designed us. We are in Him and He is in us. I love you all.

My BFF from the age of four years old, my birthday twin, Xavia Thompson. You have never changed. You have a pure heart, and I love you.

My childhood best cousins, Anitra Miller and Tiffany Durant. You are my best cousins forever. I love you both.

My godmother, Mrs. Silvia Mickens. You have always led me on a straight and narrow path. You are the real truth. I value and love our relationship. I love you.

My two precious goddaughters, Carson and Ashton Jackson. I pray that I can be the example you always need. I am always here for you two. I love you both.

Thank you, Ashley, for being my best friend for so many years. We share so many gifts in common.I love you.

Carolyn Bates you are faithful in everything you do. A best friend to me and always on time. The best Godmom to my sons .We love you always NaNa.

Toshia Snoddy thank you for being a good friend to me. You have painted me with the most beautiful paint brush . You're truly amazing. I love you Sis!

Barber Towanda Martin Posey has been a real big sister to me. She has always kept it real with much love and wisdom.

Shawn Thompson, I love your beautiful heart.Thank you for being you lovely.

I have always loved my playmates .We go back to the 80"s. Bonita ,Dawn, Towanda, Shawn C-train.

Charlie's Angels my riders! It's nothing we don't do. They have always had my front, back, and side. No matter the weather or storm, they are here for it.(Field Haven)

Uncle Waddy, Aunt Billie, Uncle Lonnie, Aunt Rosa, and Uncle Keith, thank you all for playing a part in my childhood memories. You all played a part in showing me love growing up. I love you all.

My Step Father Kieth,Father in law Strick ,brother in laws,Tony, Mark, Casey. I love you all.

A special shout out and thank you to author Brittany Smalls. She has been a huge inspiration and a great part of me completing my journey in the finishing touches of my book. A truly good friend and supporter of mine. I'm forever grateful for you. You have been so selfless and a breath of fresh air. Thank you for being so passionate about your work and your expertise. You are great.

INTRODUCTION

This book was inspired by my loving grandmother, the late Carrie Willams Miller. She was the greatest example of a fivefold woman. Her life was exceptionally blessed. The wisdom that came from her still blesses me today. I know the favor she had in her life was transferred as a gift to me. We have generational inheritance from the Kingdom of God. Everyone who came across my grandmother's path has experienced her love. You will not find a greater quality of a woman than my grandmother. I am the youngest daughter of my grandmother's only daughter, Carolyn. My grandmother had her hand on me from the very beginning of my life. In fact, we spent the first twenty years of my life together. Those years were the foundation of my life. They were the very making of me. To look back now and see what she was doing for me has meant the world to me. I have no choice but to repeat the absolute best example before me. The gifts she gave me are the ones you can't buy: her time, wisdom, love, and most of all her heart.

My grandmother, my mother, and my oldest sister (Bonita) have all been God's best to me. It took me as an adult to look back to be able to see and understand that God surrounded me early on with so much love and protection from these three. I was their baby. To be honest, I loved the fact that I was the baby. This put me in a sweet spot. They taught me so much. My first memories in life are of them. It was and still is a profound love. I will forever love and cherish them. Generations after generations will reap the rewards and benefits from these amazing women of God.

This book, *Becoming A Fivefold Madam,* is to meet women where they are in life. With God's wisdom and Spirit leading me every step of the way, I am hoping that I can add to women in many ways. I pray that when you are done with this book, you will be five times as great of a woman than before. With God's anointing and power flowing through His Holy Spirit, a fivefold madam of the Lord will be born.

I currently have two granddaughters, Jailyn and Gigi, whom I adore. I am using the hand of God in their life to help them to become young madams of God. This goes for nieces and goddaughters as well. I pray they all can receive it. A young madam comes with years of training, which was the very foundation that was given to me by my grandmother. I believe that no matter what age you are, God will meet you where you are in your journey. He will continue to grow, strengthen, and mold you. You are made in the image of God (see Genesis 1:27).

My first memory of my grandmother is sitting in her lap in the back seat of an already full car. We were riding to church with her son, his wife, and their two kids. We went to Sunday school and church every Sunday. She was already molding me into a young madam. I also have a memory of sitting in her lap in the car going to kindergarten. Before leaving, she would put lunch money in an envelope with the most beautiful cursive handwriting you will ever see. My grandmother made the best breakfast for me in the mornings before I went to school. I didn't live with her, but I was usually with her early in the mornings and late at night. Sometimes I would even stay overnight. I never missed a day at her house because I always wanted to spend time with her. When I became a teenager, we were together every Saturday morning, cleaning and prepping for Sunday dinner the next day.

This is how I got my weekend money to do fun things with my friends. To this day, cleaning and cooking come easily to me because I grew up with this as a family value. It was never a bother to me. It was all part of her unconditional love. Her words of wisdom and prayers made me feel better. She was a rewarder of any of my accomplishments. She also always guided me to spend time with the right families, so that I would have the best group of people to learn from and gain a godly way of life and thinking. She was serious about her family. She had a hand in all of us. Coming from an older generation, she had a beautiful mindset. I'm honored to be her granddaughter. She was a lily in the valley.

My grandmother cherished all of her children and their children. She was even hands-on with her great-grandchildren. If one set of parents worked the first shift and the other set of parents worked the second shift, that meant that the kids from the second shift would be over more. Also, if a parent was a single parent, my grandmother was needed more in this family. She spread love where she was needed the most at that time and season. No child was left behind. Each family needed different things, but no matter what the need was, she was sure to provide it. She was the matriarch for certain.

My cousins can tell you about her hot, buttered biscuits. Even if we were on the next street over, when she called for us, it didn't matter what was going on. We stopped what we were doing, and it was a race to get to her place. Those biscuits were homemade and fresh out of the oven, with a piece of butter in the middle. She did everything in the spirit of love. Her fried chicken was unbelievable. They were fried hard and fresh out of the pan in foil paper, and then she removed the grease from the chicken with a paper napkin. I would walk my aunt (her sister) a piece of chicken every single Thursday. My aunt loved the back piece of the chicken. She lived on the street right behind my grandmother—literally two houses behind her. That was how my grandmother was. She made sure everyone, from kids to grandkids, had their favorite piece of chicken. Not only that, but she also prepared my uncle a lunch bag with food in it every day when he worked at his second job. Everybody knew that they better not touch it. It sat in the middle of the table in a brown paper sack until he came for it. It was her way of rewarding him for being a dedicated worker. Another uncle came on Saturdays to cut the men's hair. My grandmother would then cook freshly fried hamburgers with onions southern style. Don't let me get started on her dressing or her custard pies—mercy! I'm simply happy to share how great of a cook she was. She fed the neighborhood. Even the life insurance guy or gal would eat dinner at our kitchen table. I have seen so much of her gift and ability to feed *everyone*. She fed the community. She would also sell ice cream for fifty cents to the kids in the community. It was always a fair price. She was a pillar in the community. They love and remember her to this day.

For the first three years of my oldest son's life, she was there for us. As long as she had health and strength, she would help take care of him. I had my son when I was in high school, and I went to school in the mornings and worked in the evenings. My seventy-year-old grandmother, along with my grandad, went and got my son from the sitter daily, and she would keep him until I got off at night. She even helped me on the weekends so I could have a break. They would be sitting up in the den waiting for me. My grandmother and her sister would call him Judson Mills. They were tickled by him. She always said he was her little preacher boy.

She also loved me to do her hair, and she wouldn't let anybody else touch it. After I had the baby, she would come to my house and sit on a pillow on the floor so I could roll her hair. People would often ask her if they could help, but she would simply say no and shake her head from side to side. I love how she felt about me when it came to her hair and style. That's how serious this was. My grandmother also helped my cousin with her son. Our sons were close in age, and she would keep both of them at the same time. He would be there often in the evenings as well. My nephew loved her pancakes so much. He has warm memories of her as well. Let me remind you, these are her *great-grand-children*. My grandmother was a generation-to-generation-to-generation blessing. She loved unconditionally through the toughest times in her life.

My grandmother never became an empty nester. Her two youngest sons stayed with her, and she took care of them to the end. Her plate was always full, but that was never an excuse for her. She was so strong. She was a giver to everyone. I'm sure that everyone who knew her has their own special and unique story to tell about her.

My sister was her first grandchild. They had an incredibly special bond. She raised her in the home from birth. She protected and loved her dearly. My sister always wrapped my grandmother's Christmas gifts, but when she got older and became an adult, she didn't have the time to do it anymore. So wrapping the gifts became my job. My sister and I are nine years apart, so I had the time for it. Believe me, my grandmother had a thousand gifts to wrap—gifts for the children, grandchildren, a ton of people from her church, for everybody. One time, she gave me an extra gift to wrap for my sister for Christmas. I said to myself, *what?* She looked at my face and saw the disappointment. She said, "Does your sister know about the Air Jordans that I bought for you a few months ago?" Well, that changed my expression, and I giggled. Those shoes were a hundred dollars back in 1992. They were my first pair of Jordans. They were all black and had some red and a splash of purple. It was another example of her spreading love around. If you got more attention, it was because you needed it the most at that time. She gave good measures of her love to all of us. Because of her, I now understand that every situation isn't the same and shouldn't be handled the same. It makes so much more sense now.

As I became a young adult, she would tell me to let my sister wear my clothes when she asked for them. She would hear my sister asking and me saying no. How unfair, right? What I didn't mention is that when I was in middle school, I would ask my sister to wear her stuff, and sometimes she would let me. So it's like my grandmother was teaching me that we needed each other at various times for different things. She was teaching us to be there for one another. Since she was older, my sister naturally took care of me. As the younger sister, I didn't have those natural instincts, so my grandmother was instilling them in me early on. At the time I didn't understand this, but it is clear and obvious now. My grandmother would be proud to see our relationship today. She was close to her sister, and my sister and I tease each other often saying she is Carrie and I'm Aunt "Baby." We fit the description seriously.

My grandmother gave my two youngest cousins the most beautiful handmade matching church dresses, which she often did for them. She gave them this for Christmas. It was different from what the other grand-kids got. The others got money, but it was age-appropriate for them because they were older grandkids. She perfectly measured her love for all of us. I really enjoyed wrapping those gifts. Seven years later my job of wrapping gifts was done, and my grandmother wanted me to train my younger cousin. Sad to say, that was her last year. She became ill and the doctor gave her six months to live. She went home to be with the Lord on December 2, 1998. Thankfully, she was able to witness two blessings before she passed. Earlier in that same year, my oldest niece was born. After that, she got to go to the one thing I can say she was proud of: my wedding. She had a little veil on her head, and it was so cute on her. My friends said to me, "Your grandmother is getting married too." It was the sweetest thing ever. It was a delightful day for our family. She loved my husband, Garnell, so much. She was so tickled by the way he wrapped me in his arms and danced with me so romantically at the reception. She knew then that we had true love. When the reception was over, we went home to change our clothes. We ended up at her house to talk about the wedding. She said her only regret was not having a big dinner. We had finger foods, but that was me trying to be cautious with the price. I didn't even give her and my grandad the choice. I was grateful for them being there for me and taking on a responsibility financially in my wedding.

I tell you today that the foundation was laid for me. This has really sustained me. We will recycle this family bloodline of madams. But it's not only for my family. It's for whoever wants it and receives it. Spirit to spirit, generation to generation. That's what kind of God we serve. A loving God who stays the same. "Tell it to your children, and let your children tell it to their children, and their children to the next generation" (Joel 1:3).

My prayer to our Heavenly Father.
Heavenly and gracious Father, I come boldly before your throne of grace, asking for your blessing to write this book. My purpose is to be a witness for your Kingdom. My vision is for women from all over the world to become five times as great as the women that she was before reading this book. Through your words, wisdom, power, strength, anointing, courage, compassion, and love, Lord, when she is done, she will walk as a madam of the Lord. Proverbs 31:29 says, "Many women do noble things, but you surpass them all." God, I pray for the anointing that I have received from you. Let it always remain in me. As the Word of God declares, teach me with all deep levels of knowl-

edge and with an anointing of the Holy Spirit who searches all things. God, give me wisdom and keep me firmly planted in the truth of your word. I pray for your knowledge and continued discernment. Psalm 46:5 says, "God is within her, she will not fall."

All praises to you, Father. Thank you for changing me, molding me, and teaching me. Thank you, Lord, for never giving up on me. Thank you for being a forgiving God again and again. Thank you for your new mercies every morning. I cover my family and self in the precious blood of Jesus. No weapon formed against us shall prosper. In Jesus' name I pray. Amen.

The very hand of God is working in your life, which is the beginning of being transformed and redeemed in Christ.

Your thumb represents becoming a daughter of God. Your index finger represents becoming a wife. Your middle finger represents becoming a mother. Your ring finger represents the ministry. Your pinky finger represents becoming a businesswoman.

CHAPTER 1

YOU—A DAUGHTER REPRESENTING THE THUMB. IT HOLDS POWER!

You were created by our Almighty Father Jehovah-Jireh. He knows you by name. Before you were ever conceived, He knew you. You were born as a daughter. Your calling is to be a daughter of God. This is your destiny and future. You can't choose your parents. You were born into a family, and it was their job to train and help develop you as a daughter—preferably as a young daughter of God. Sometimes life happens, and it's evident that not everyone had this type of upbringing. The good news is that it's *not over!* Some families come differently. Not everyone comes from a two-parent household. It doesn't mean that you are less than. Even so, you need your mom and dad to both contribute to your life. However that looks, you need them to develop you. Don't let this concern you. Things may not be in order. This doesn't mean you can't have the life that God sees for you. God has the final say. God looks at your heart, and He

1

will use your suffering for good. God can use suffering to develop us into better people (see Romans 5:3-5).

My life was disorganized and in disorder from early on. This made things difficult, but in the end, it actually made me stronger because of my struggle. I can tell you that it took me a while. Once I invited the Holy Spirit in my life, I was never the same. I became a woman of God. This led me to becoming the fivefold madam that my grandmother was growing me to be. Everything came from the hand of God, working in me even as a child. My grandmother was a willing vessel, directing me as a woman to accept Him as my Lord and Savior. The covering of my precious grandmother molded me and trained me with biblical beliefs. Your invitation today is to become an established woman of God. If you are working on it, no matter where you are in your walk with God, He wants to upgrade you. He wants to bring more value to your life. Madam of the Lord, praise Him in advance. Thank you, Lord, Hallelujah.

Let's pray.

Father, I pray for every daughter who reads this book. I pray that she receives you and becomes a daughter of Christ, and that she will forever be transformed by your grace and mercy. She is called to be fivefold madam, being five times as great of a woman as she was. I decree and declare that she becomes a fivefold madam. Please heal her heart from all past hurts, whether from her biological father, stepfather, grandfather, uncle, past boyfriends, current boyfriend, past husband, current husband—or any other man that has ever hurt her. I pray for your healing and peace to come into her heart. Give her a pure heart. Renew her spirit. Transform her mind as she reads. I pray for deliverance in every area needed. She will never be the same. She will know her value, her worth, and her place in your Kingdom. Remake her from the crown of her head to the soles of her blessed feet. In the mighty name of Jesus, come forth, lady of the Lord. A fivefold madam will be born. If you believe it, shout, "Hallelujah," and thank Jesus. He is the reason we can be redeemed. We are saved by the precious blood of Jesus. Amen.

God will not only break you to remake you, but he will also rename you. In other words, before God blesses you, he will change your very identity (see Romans 6:4).

Let's look at the hand. In Ezra 7:28 it says, "Because the hand of the Lord my God was on me, I took courage." God's invisible and intangible hand is also on you: leading, guiding, encouraging, protecting, strengthening, and giving you courage.

Thumb (Power)

Your thumb is a symbol of power, protection, and character. Let's talk first about the power you have being a fivefold madam. There is power in you; it's time to activate it, accept it, and perform it! God has given you power. Power can be many things. The power that the Holy Spirit gives us is a gift, like the boldness to teach the gospel and the power to perform healings. These are just some of God's gifts. We all have gifts. I encourage you to find out what your gifts are from the Lord.

As God's children, we all have been called to live beyond what goes on in the natural world while still living in this world. When the Lord Jesus calls us, He gives us power and authority to do the work of His ministry. Jesus received this great authority because of His obedience. To this day, those who follow Him in obedience have power from God. Luke 10:19 says, "Behold, I give you the authority to trample on serpents and scorpions, and over all the power of the enemy and nothing shall by any means heart you."

Madam, it's up to you to be obedient. Move when God says to. Will you sit on your power? Will you walk in it? I pray that you do, because someone needs you. Not all women know him. Be honored that you do and are His daughter. And if you don't know him yet, this is your invitation to grow in him. You are reading the right book. Your circle of women should be like you are. Remember, not everyone can go where you are going. If you end up in a new circle, be glad you outgrew it. Go out to the world so that someone else sees your light. They need to see Jesus in you. Matthew 5:16 says, "In the same way, let your light shine before others, that they may see your good deeds and glorify your Father in heaven.."

The more women that can walk with Him, the more pleasing it is to God our Father in Heaven. Daughters are a true blessing from God (see Psalm 127:3). They bring love, joy, and fulfillment to their families. Shout out to women! We are spectacular!

God sees His daughters as worthy of love. You, His daughter, are worthy of His love simply because He made you and you are His! God will love you as a woman no matter what. He will forgive you and use you for His Kingdom. Thank you, Gracious Father. The heart of a godly woman is like a deep pool of compassion willing to help those in need. In the book of Ruth, Naomi was a broken-hearted woman. She suffered much pain and famine and she lost her husband. She went through it all. Ruth was drawn to Naomi and the God she served, and it was Ruth's compassion that got her favor with Naomi. This brought favor upon her, and she became a wife to Boaz and a faithful daughter-in-law to Naomi. Depending on your situation, God calls you to either be a Naomi for a young Ruth or a young Ruth for a Naomi.

Naomi is an example of a restored mother. God restored the losses in Naomi's life, and you can trust Him to restore the losses in your life as well. As women, we have all kinds of challenges in our world. Every great

BECOMING A FIVEFOLD MADAM

person who changed had to go through something and let the power of God transform them first. I am a witness to every single hurt that changed me. Pressure creates diamonds. As a woman, at some point, you will experience pain and pressure. It comes down to what you do with it. If God allowed it, then it was for your good. Take a minute and praise God for the power He has given you and the ability to transform you. This is a true and righteous gift from our Father. What greater love will you ever know?

Madam of the Lord, it is so important to walk in His power and anointing in your life. God desires this for you. Love using your gifts and staying in the Lord's presence. This brings God's protection upon your life and your family. The shield of faith protects us with His promises. He will order His angels to protect you wherever you go. God will command angels to guard you with twenty-four-hour protection. God has given His angels the authority to act on you. Archangel Michael, the most powerful war angel, will fight for you. See Psalm 91 for a scripture of divine protection. Pray and confess this scripture daily.

Let's pray together.

Dear Lord, please protect this beautiful blossoming madam with your divine protection. Shield her from all evil. Command your angels to watch over her day and night. Release war angel Micheal to fight every single battle known and unknown. I thank you and praise you for this special gift of protection. I have faith as a fivefold madam that you will do exceedingly and abundantly more than I could ever ask. I live in your protection and stay in the shadow of you, Lord. Almighty and powerful Lord, thank you for keeping her safe from secret traps that are known and unknown. I have faith and know that she is secure in you. In the name of Jesus. Amen.

God's focus is not on condemning you but on healing and restoring you. God did not send his son into the world to condemn the world, but to save the world through him (see John 3:17-19). You have the power to make, create, choose, and build who you are. Your character, integrity, and honesty are a choice. Learn from wrong choices and don't stay there. Your character is your background. You get to choose how you present yourself as a woman, the friends you have, and the way you dress in public. You are called to be set apart and be different. Sometimes you will lose family and friends. Stay in your calling and do what He is calling you to. God is a rewarder. Obedience is better than sacrifice.

A woman of substance is called to hold power, positive influence, and meaning. You can be a branded woman of immense importance and accomplishments. By *brand* I mean excellent quality and personality (see Proverbs 31). You are rare. A fivefold madam brings light to the dark places for others. If you are reading this book, God has a gift for you. Allow and receive God to pour his anointing over your life and through your life. Invite His Holy Spirit in. He is a teacher of so many things. If you are already anointed, receive a double portion. I decree and declare that you are a woman of God. I decree and declare that you are becoming a fivefold madam of the Lord. Your thinking is changing. You are honored in Him with mercy and grace.

What is a Fivefold Madam of the Lord?

Primarily, it is being a daughter of God. Secondarily, it is being a wife, mother, godmother, mother figure, sister, aunt, friend, woman with gifts in ministry, businesswoman, and woman of great importance and value. "She is more precious than rubies; nothing you desire can compare with her" (Proverbs 3:15). You are an anointed woman with many spiritual gifts and qualities of the Lord. They call you blessed.

If you accept being a madam of the Lord, confess that you are by saying, "I am a fivefold madam of the Lord."

Put   your   name   right   here:

———————————————————

I will be five times as great of a woman. I receive God's blessings and power in my life. Thank you, Lord, for giving me your strength, power, and anointing me to be this madam of honor. In Jesus' name, Amen!

Your lineage is what comes before you and after you. The steps of a God-fearing woman, my grandmother, came before me. Those seeds she planted before me are generational. The seeds I plant today are for my little madams that shall be birthed into a fivefold madam of the Lord. Watering those seeds are words spoken over them. What am I teaching them? What am I showing them? Who has God called you to be that example for? Who has he assigned to you? Be an active role in who the Lord has given to you. Your daughters, granddaughters, nieces, goddaughters, and neighbors' daughters need you in their lives. Being a daughter of God brings many qualities. Not only do younger people need you, but sometimes your sister needs you as well. We are called to be sisters that are friends.

Take a moment to reflect. Write down your thoughts as a daughter of God. Study your answers. Focus on what you don't want to work on. One thing is for sure: times change and people change, but our Father has stayed the same yesterday and forever.

1. How do you see yourself?

2. What's your identity? Who are you?

3. Are you where you want to be in your life?

4. What can you do to make yourself greater? Do you have goals and plans on paper? Are your dreams and visions written down? Are you praying over these things?

5. What qualities do you have like Ruth had when she gained favor with Naomi? Hers was compassion. What can you do to make it a stronger quality of yours?

6. Do you feel loved by God?

Father God, thank you for this beautiful madam of yours. I pray that you, Lord, open her spiritual eyes so she can see her true beauty from the inside out. Open her heart so she can receive you as Lord. Let her receive every precious gift you have for her. Let her heart be free in you and be led by your Spirit. Her spiritual ears are open; she hears your voice with no confusion. Her past is her past, and she will not look back on anything. She is creating a new future. Give her your supernatural power to help change lives. Let her follow you and spend intimate time with you to hear your plans. She is growing daily, and the ones around her are growing. In Jesus' name. Amen.

(see Ephesians 4:22-24)

CHAPTER 2

A WIFE!

The pointer or index finger represents a wife. It is about leadership, authority, and self-esteem, as well as holding authority and power. This finger wins.

Becoming a wife is a complete blessing from God. Don't let anyone take you from this precious gift when it's time. You are God's daughter. He birthed you through your natural parents. Now it is a new season to become a wife. You leave your parents and cleave to your husband (see Genesis 2:24). Proverbs 12:4 says, "A wife of noble character is her husband's crown, but a disgraceful wife is like decay in his bones."

Single madams, you may be called to be single for a season. You are waiting on God. You are married to Him. He makes all things sufficient for you.

Becoming a wife requires you to be a complete person. This means that you are not broken or damaged. Sometimes dating and deeply caring for the wrong person can scar you. These are some of the questions you want to ask yourself before you marry.

1. Am I hurt by past relationships with a potential mate or ex-mate?

2. Am I healed from past hurts from my first love or my father? If not, seek counsel and get the help that you need to heal. Pray and ask our Father to heal you. Ask him to show you what steps to take in your process.

3. Ask God if this is the man He has for you. Just because you love him doesn't mean he is the one God has for you. Just because he asked you, doesn't mean he is the one.

4. How does he make you feel? Is he gentle with you? Does he make you feel like you can trust him? Pay close attention to how he treats you.

5. Is he a man of God that has your same beliefs and faith? Does he fear God? Does he have a foundation in God? Are y'all equally yoked?

Equally yoked means to be joined with the someone of same belief system. 2 Corinthians 6:14 says that we must not be yoked together with those who do not believe. We should have the same beliefs and values.

Find a good marriage counselor before you marry. Everything that is good is prepared for. These are all things to protect you and your spouse before you say *I do*. A healthy relationship takes patience, time, and energy. We, as madams of the Lord, have all the wisdom we need in our Father before we enter into marriage. Be on guard, pray, and watch what the Father shows you. No one is perfect, but we are working on being great.

Forgiveness

Forgive your biological father or any adult male who inflicted past hurts. You can't bring that baggage into your new relationship as a wife. Don't be a victim, and don't be prone to pick the wrong men because of your father. This can result in you creating unhealthy relationships in your life. It is hard for you to grow and think if you're still in bondage from the past. You're more likely to keep attracting the same guy with just a different face. To build you up as a woman and to help heal you mentally, you're going to need individual counseling. When a person leaves your life, always learn the lesson behind it. Some of you had a good dad who lived with you, but he just didn't give you enough time. That created a void in you as a woman that you might try and fill, as this has made you vulnerable. If you don't deal with it, you could end up picking the wrong guy. It could be that your father treated another sibling differently than you when you were growing up. He might not have spent the time with you that you wanted and needed. He may have always moved in a different direction in life than you wanted. For instance, perhaps you wanted to be a ballet dancer, but he responded with a frown, saying that he wanted you to be a basketball player because you're tall. These are feelings that you grow with and hold onto as a child. Or maybe your dad was a habitual cheater, constantly hurting your mom. The outcome of this may be that you swore you would never marry. Dads can hurt their daughters in many ways, and it will still affect you as an adult woman.

Stop and ask God if you have unresolved father issues from your birth father, stepfather, or other father figure who had access to your life as a child. If so, ask Him to show these issues to you. Anything deep or hidden must be pulled up at the root and dealt with.

Father God, in Jesus' name, please heal this madam from all past hurts from her father or any other male adult. In the name of Jesus, we renounce every negative word spoken over her. We ask that you touch your daughter and heal her heart, body, mind, and soul from all forms of abuse. I pray that she forgives those who hurt her. I pray that you bring her godly counsel and help her heal and move on step by step. Let her be bold and call out those things that need to be dealt with. We ask by your power that you provide her with wisdom and strength. She will be healed and live a healthy lifestyle. She will choose wisely who she lets in her life. She will learn from every lesson that comes her way. She will keep you at the center of every decision made in her love life. Believe and receive, madam of the Lord! In the powerful and mighty name of Jesus! Amen.

When you get married, you leave your first family and move on to your second family, namely your husband and eventually your children. We love order, but sometimes it doesn't always happen in order. We have blended families. That is okay too! What I do know is that God loves you. There is no mistake that can keep Him from loving you. If you are human, you are going to make a mistake. What did you learn from it? Getting good at mistakes and learning from them means growth.

I have been married for twenty-five years. It didn't come easy. There were years of wrong thinking and behavior. My husband and I didn't always say *I do*. But God has always been at the root of us, no matter the storm—and believe me, there have been some storms. After all, the world has a way of challenging you. But in the end, we always came out with a rainbow. We married young. He was twenty and I was nineteen. We both had intense feelings for one another, and we knew what we wanted. We just weren't equipped for what all the world had in store for us. When it's a snowstorm, you need equipment to travel on the roads. If not, you will be stuck. Same goes for marriage. Evil will try and come against you. What I do know is that no weapon formed against my marriage will prosper (see Isaiah 54:17). We stand today on that word. My husband came from his household, and I came from mine, but we came together as one. We both had trauma growing up, but we felt safe with one another. We both had experienced the world and knew what that was like, and we found comfort in one another. As it turned out, what we had was rare, young, and real, but we did not yet have the tools we needed in our marriage.

We went through two separations out of twenty-five years, but God turned those around and blessed us with two vow renewals. The first vow renewal was seven years after our wedding, and it took place on a mountaintop. Our second vow renewal was on our twenty-fifth wedding anniversary, which took place in Hawaii on the beach! We said our renewals in Hawaiian language and culture. For every storm, there has always been a rainbow. The new tools God blessed us with were the gifts of wisdom and knowledge. That came with age and time, alongside a marriage counselor with God's values.

Marriage seminars, retreats, and married couples are God's gifts to a married couple. God will always give you what you need to weather any storm. He will never leave or forsake you. These are the very things that make you the best and greatest person you can be. God will use life experiences to shape us and help us grow. When we become mature and complete, not lacking anything, we are able to make a difference in the lives around us (see 1 Timothy 4:16). Our pains are supposed to lead us closer to God and expose what is really inside of us. Losing my precious grandmother on earth at twenty years old was my most traumatic and heartbreaking experience. I went straight to God our Father. God took the absolute best from this world. My only comfort was the life she lived and who she belonged to. I know I will see her again one day.

Love your loved ones while they are here on earth. We all have to take that heavenly appointment one day, and you want to be able to say you were the best madam and wife you could possibly be. My personal experience is that a three-stranded cord is not easily broken, which is a cord of three strands that become braided or intertwined together. This type of cord is difficult to break. One strand represents the bride, one represents the groom, and the other represents God. With these things tying and bonding you together as one, you can survive. This is a powerful symbol of unity, strength, and faith. A person standing alone can be attacked and defeated, but two can stand back-to-back and conquer. Three are even better, for a triple-braided cord is not easily broken (see Ecclesiastes 4:12). This is another tool my husband and I were blessed with to sustain our marriage. As a madam of the Lord, your prayer language needs to be constant every day. If you are already married, pray for your mate. If you are single, pray for the mate that you haven't met yet.

Father, please listen to my prayers today. I pray for marriages to be healed, to be delivered and set free, and to be restored better than their original state. God, you know what this madam needs in her marriage. God, I pray that you perfect her marriage. Send her and her husband godly couples to connect with. Give this madam wisdom on how to be a loyal and fruitful wife. Give her the desire to keep herself beautiful inside and out. Let her have strength and be a helpful mate to her husband. I pray that her husband will honor her and cherish her all the days of her life. Let there be the right connections for the single madam so she can receive the spouse you wish. Open her spiritual ears and eyes. Keep her from all harm and everything that's not for her. Give her wisdom on how to be ready when you send him. In the name of Jesus! Amen.

In the same way, you husbands must give honor to your wives (see 1 Peter 3:7). Treat your wife with understanding as you live together. She is your equal partner in God's gift of new life. Treat her as you should, so your prayers won't be hindered. A husband's prime responsibility is to protect his wife from danger, whether it is physical, mental, emotional, or psychological. He must make his wife feel secure in his presence.

Many years ago, my husband and I were going on a trip and were almost out of gas. He wanted to keep going, but the GPS took us on another route and the area wasn't familiar, so I wasn't sure how long it would be before another station. I told him my concerns, and he brushed me off and kept driving. He thought

I was going to still talk and have a good time, but I froze up and didn't talk. He passed another gas station, and then finally stopped at the third station. Once he fueled up and got back in the car, I told him I didn't feel safe and secure. As a man, he was supposed to make me feel safe, and he didn't. He apologized and told me that he realized that he had messed up the rhythm of our conversation. My angry feelings left me, and the entire atmosphere changed when he acknowledged this. Remember to always care about what your partner wants and needs. Put them first. Being selfless saves your marriage. Respect your spouse's feelings on how something makes them feel, even if you don't understand.

Single madams, if you don't feel this, my advice would be to wait on marriage. You could be dating your future husband right now, but that doesn't mean you are ready to be married. That's okay too. It's better to prepare for it. My sixteen-year-old son has been practicing driving since he was thirteen years old. At fifteen, he got his permit and was able to practice with other vehicles on the road. Then, at sixteen, he was finally able to take the test for his license to make it legal. He grew into this. It didn't happen overnight. We didn't rush him at all. Something worth having takes preparation. Taking your time to get married is a sign of maturity. Whether you have a biological father, stepfather, or husband, God is your source. He is your Heavenly Father. He completes all things. Know who you are and who you belong to. No need to look for your Boaz. He will find you at the right time and season. In the meantime, make yourself beautiful in all things. Your journey should be filled with beautiful things. Work on yourself mentally and pamper yourself physically. Remember that what's for you will always find you. Single madams, God adores you. Cinderella's story tells you that no matter your status in life, if the shoe fits, it's for you.

No one can keep you from getting what's for you. By the power vested in us by the Almighty God, through the Holy Spirit, we can positively change the world. When we force the shoe, we end up with something God didn't attend. This causes unnecessary trauma and pain. What God has for you, will be. Don't force that shoe; let it be the right fit. Even though a relationship is over, that doesn't mean it is. Separate yourself from soul ties. Ungodly soul ties will leave you with low self-esteem. It will have you bound. It's impossible to attract your guy (the guy that's really for you) if these things are attached to you. Pray that God removes

BECOMING A FIVEFOLD MADAM

the entanglement and frees you from the individual. He has the power to do this. You have to want this. Cleanse yourself with the Word of God. Bring Him your confession, and ask Him to untie it and release you from it. Give in to your Father's plan to be healed. God's desire is for you to be in a happy and healthy relationship with Him as the center (see Ephesians 3:20).

Married women, cherish your husband and allow him to lead. Be his helpmate (see Genesis 2:18). Every house runs differently. Find out what works for yours. Establish that and make sure you commit to it. As a wife, I am more traditional. This was the example set for me by my grandmother. It fits and works for me. With my husband's upbringing, this fits him as well. We are a great match. My husband reminds me of my grandfather, Waddy, in so many ways. One of the things is that they are both the sign of Aries. They also have the same personalities. The myth is every woman who gets married ends up marrying the man she admired as a child, the man she looked up to and respected the most. It could be their dad, grandfather, uncle, or someone else entirely. For me, that man was my grandfather. My husband even walks tall like him. When I met him for the first time, this was the first

27

thing I noticed about him. I saw him walking from a distance, and I was drawn from that very moment. We have a traditional lifestyle, similar to the example set before me by my grandparents. From early on, we had an understanding that yard work was his, and I cleaned our house inside. As we got older, he added cooking, laundry, and dishes, and sometimes things changed for the better. For so long, I was a stay-at-home mom. We changed as our lives change. Even with that, we have set the reset button a couple of times. We grew from past mistakes and challenges. The lesson is to grow together in all things. Big or small, God must be in the center. Invite the Holy Spirit into your marriage.

God has given us great purposes for marriage. One thing is companionship. God's principle was to create Eve to help meet Adam's need for a companion (see Genesis 2:18). Companionship is spending quality time, growing closer, and enjoying shared activities. This is an emotional need that brings forth intimacy.

Another gift would be redemption. Redemption means to regain something that has been lost. The strongest relationships face challenges. Christ will and can redeem your marriage. He will make it better than before (see Ephesians 5:22-23).

I am a witness. I have been in a relationship for twenty-eight years and married for twenty-five years. God surely redeemed our marriage. He made our marriage stronger. As individuals, we are better than before. All the pain and trauma we endured made us stronger together. After every storm, there is a rainbow.

Father, please anoint this madam's marriage. Destroy every yoke of bondage. Her marriage will be healed and hope will return. Everything that the enemy tried to lock up shall be released. I ask you to redeem her marriage. Bring love and light back. Let her marriage be full of companionship. Let her marriage be designed and working in the healthy way you called it to be. In the name of Jesus, we praise your name, Father. Enjoy the gift of being a wife. I pray for blessings over your marriages. Amen.

"Let the morning bring me word of your unfailing love, for I have put my trust in you. Show me the way I should go, for to you I entrust my life. Rescue me from my enemies, Lord, for I hide myself in you. Teach me to do your will, for you are my God; may your good Spirit lead me on level ground" (Psalm 143:8-10).

Marriage

Your marriage can go through various stages and seasons, but your prayers change things. Redirect your steps. There is always room for improvement in your marriage. There's always room for growth. Find a marriage support group. Go on marriage retreat seminars. This can be a nice getaway for the weekend while you work on building your marriage. This is also a way to get questions answered and to get prayers and covering over your marriage. The anointing heals marriages. Stay connected with the vine, with Jesus, our true source of life. It's where our need to survive and flourish comes from.

One major problem my husband and I had was that he liked to stay out visiting people. He didn't like to be at home. He was always on the go. He didn't have a hobby, but he loved to socialize, especially when we were in our twenties. This used to hurt our marriage. The bond wasn't there and the family wasn't benefiting from this. He didn't see the value like he does now. His thinking changed so he changed. He grew from an old way of thinking. We have a new generation of kids at home, and they are benefiting from this change. I'm thankful for my husband growing from this and making the best decision. Family is a priority. Now we see that yesterday's problems are no longer today's issues. Praise God! God is triumphant, and there is power in that! I'm not perfect. I had to change some things as well, like being a shopper 24/7. I thank God I'm better than before.

The honeymoon phase is an early part of a relationship that makes things so easy. You love easily and you're so happy. Your intimacy is on a deeper level. My mom used to joke with me and say, "Don't take the honey out of the moon." You need to get skilled in the rough times. Rebellion will try and set in. Not having communication in a marriage is the worst thing you can do. This causes division. It leaves a door open for the enemy to come in. The enemy will feed you lies. He wants you to grow apart. Prove him wrong and let him know you will fight for your marriage with the Word of God, getting rid of all stubbornness.

I only know how to keep it real. I was always told to tell the truth and shame the devil, so I'm coming to you in truth. Temptation is real and roaming this earth. To resist the enemy and his tactics, you will need the Word of God living inside of you. Don't slip in your thoughts and feelings. Your reality is your marriage. You already have the greatest gift. Do your homework with your spouse. Watch each other and know each other's love language. Have talks and communicate what you like. Make those things a priority. Take one thing and master it. Then start with another one. Celebrate and congratulate your spouse when they do something good in life. This is a partnership that is based on a friendship first. Be best friends. Be on the same wave pattern with your thoughts. Great minds think alike. This is a team that you are building. You started at the bottom and worked your way to the top together. I was always told that two is better than one.

Romance

The 777 rule is a great rule to live by. The first seven is to go on a date every seven days. When kids come into play, the date might be in your backyard or on your lunch break while wearing your work uniforms. My husband will come and get me after work with his uniform on, and we get quality time in. The second seven is to go away for a night every seven weeks. It can be local. My husband and I went away for a night in Greenville, SC, which is our hometown. We love this. It's absolutely amazing. The final seven is to go on a romantic weekend getaway every seven months. Keep things exciting and new. Women, get some new lingerie, something that you want to put on at night that is appealing to your mate and that is something he hasn't seen at home. Make yourself attractive at night-time. It's important to go nightgown shopping for your regular nights at home as well. Try new fragrances from time to time. Change your hairstyle sometimes. If he doesn't have a pet name for you, give yourself one and refer to yourself by that name. My husband has a lot for me. He has a pet name that he can say in front of the kids, but he also has a few for the bedroom. It's all about fun and keeping the fire burning. My mom's generation says that you shouldn't take the honey out of the moon. My generation says that you should stay lit.

Power in Agreement

When my husband and I were at a marriage retreat, we met a married couple, and the wife gave us the best advice. We already knew about this, but we were not practicing it at that time. She said to start touching and agreeing with one another. Ever since then, we have been doing this more often. We join our hands and pray for our relationship with God, marriage, children, finances, business, etc. We do not pray for these things separately, because when you become married you become one (see Mark 10:8-9).

God will flourish your marriage. He will grow your marriage into a healthy state. Water your marriage with the Word of God. This will bring the presence of God upon you. Put your marriage in God's hands and ask for God's nourishment and light. It creates friend-ships in marriages. Set goals on how to be connected spiritually and physically. God designed marriages for us to enjoy. This is a precious gift, so we should treat it specially. Be in agreement with God about your com-mitment to your spouse. Share your life together, in the good and not-so-good times. The not-so-good is what builds your relationship and makes you stronger. The most precious gift a wife can give to her husband is to love, support, and appreciate him. Spend quality time together, show interest in his interests, and be present in the moment. The number one thing that hurts a marriage is *dishonesty*. Be honest in all things. The truth hurts sometimes, but a lie destroys. Be honest in finances, your feelings, or just the truth of what happened. Don't allow distractions or people around you to keep you from being one with your spouse. Marriage is work, but agree to make it easy. Even children can distract you if you allow them. I come against the spirit of division in Jesus' name. Division can destroy a marriage.

Leviathan is the spirit of separation. This spirit saw an open door in my marriage. He used this to come in through sin. Pressure came and our entire world changed. The pain and loss pierced and wounded my marriage. The book of Job teaches us more about Leviathan. Satan asked God's permission to take Job's wealth, health, and family. This brought Job desperate pain (see Job 3:8). The thing that keeps us from being healed and restored after loss is pride and self-righteousness. What was ruling my marriage didn't change until we admitted, confessed, and truly got delivered and then healed from it. The spirit separated my marriage and family for three years. You can imagine the damage it caused. God allowed this to bring us back together stronger and healthier. Today, we don't look back. What made us better is complete *honesty*. The spirit was defeated by the *truth*. We walked in humility. This is freedom from pride or arrogance. Simply being humble. "Humility is the fear of the Lord" (Proverbs 22:4). Have a mindset like Christ.

Once we got out of the way of ourselves, God showed up with all power in his hands. He restored our marriage. We knew this was only a miracle from Him. We had to be in a place and position to receive it. During those three years, God was pruning and working all along. Manifestation came when we were ready to receive it. Don't you dare take the chicken out of the frying pan until it's ready. This goes for anything! Make sure it's the right time and season (see Ecclesiastes 3:1-8). The old life we had needed to die, only to be reborn again through Christ Jesus. This was needed to reconcile and save our family. Our hearts and the kids' hearts are smiling and beating again. God protected, transformed, restored, revived, preserved, delivered, healed, cured, rebuilt, mended, perfected, and set free. Hallelujah! Thank you, Jesus! God says, "I will restore them because I have compassion on them" (Zechariah 10:6) and "I will repay you for the years the locusts have eaten" (Joel 2:25). Yes, my God did all of this! If He did it for my marriage, he can do it for yours.

We lost a lot, but it took us to be in agreement to become free. We both were on a dark road going separate ways. We had an eighteen-year marriage established before the roads split. We were missing a lot, but the main reason was honesty. We knew God and served every Sunday service. Until we completely agreed and were honest about bad decisions and unhealthy habits, we were going to have a problem. This wasn't God's best for our life. It had to come to an end eventually. At the bottom of the pit, while we were going through the process, God never took His loving hands off of us. We had to go through the fire (see Psalm 91). When we came out, we were never going to be the same. With broken hearts and all the damage that had broken us, we knew right then how to agree with one another. When we looked into each other's eyes, we felt a new love and appreciation. It was unapologetically clear that we belonged together and were meant to be. It didn't destroy us, it *changed* us.

Dear Father, I pray for these marriages. If there is a separation, I ask that you restore the marriage back to them. If there are thoughts of separation, I pray for redirection and forgiveness. I pray for the Holy Spirit's fire to bring new passion to marriages. Let stubbornness and unforgiveness depart. Enrich in their marriages love, unity, honesty, and grace. Lord, we invite you to redirect, heal, deliver, and set free every spirit that will try and bring division. We speak to the Leviathan spirit and demand he let go of these marriages. He has no power or place in this marriage. I pray that these marriages are covered in the blood of Jesus. They will remain faithful, truthful, loyal, compassionate, loving, caring, and honest to their spouse. God, let them put you first in *everything* that they do. I pray that there will be order in their marriage. Let them grow, flourish, and multiply together. I destroy anything that will try and stand between me and my prayers right now. In Jesus' name I pray. Amen.

CHAPTER 3

A MOTHER

The next finger is your middle finger, the strongest finger. The middle finger traditionally represents responsibility, balance, and the soul. This finger represents you being a mother. If you haven't put on your full armor of God, it's time now (see Ephesians 6:10). Becoming a mother is one of the most precious gifts God can give you. As a mother, you are to nurture and protect your children. The moment you conceive, all unhealthy habits must stop. What you put in your body changes. You eat healthier. You do everything healthier. Why? Because you love this little life more than your own life. You have been given a natural superpower when it comes to your children. God trusted you to carry the seed. The seed the man gives you is planted inside of a woman to grow. That says a whole lot about women. The seed grows inside of a woman. The bond between a mother and child is undeniably strong. In the animal world, mess with a mother's babies, and the mama bear will tear you from limb to limb. Even a bird will peck you with no remorse to protect her eggs in that nest. You now have a family. You will need to protect your family. A warrior woman is strong in the Lord, in the power of God's might. She stands in her armor against the wiles of the devil (see Ephesians 6:10-18). We women must be warriors for our families. There must be no room for worries at all. We must be warriors!

God has called you to be a strong, prayerful, and stable madam, who is mission-minded and battle-ready. To be a great warrior madam, you must know how to recognize the enemy. If you have a son, we are praying that he becomes a mighty man of valor. As for your daughter, we are praying that she becomes a virtuous woman warrior who's a madam of the Lord. We teach our children how to be spirit-filled. We train them in the way they should go, and when they are old they will not depart from this. An enemy is roaming, and he wants nothing more than your precious seeds. Our faith is in God. He is our shield, help, defender, and deliverer. Instruct your young children, and when they are adults, continue to teach them. I strongly recommend that you train your adult children. They will always need your love, prayers, and support. Never give up on your seeds. No matter what, you are called to cover your children. How? Call upon the Lord to build a security system around your children (see Zachariah 2:5). The blood of Jesus creates a bloodline around your children. Call upon your child's guardian angels to protect them. Speak it out of your mouth, confess it, pray it. Cover them with God's promises—His love, protection, and presence. Isaiah 44:3 says that God's Spirit is covering my children like the sky covers the earth. Blessings from God are upon me and my children.

Being a parent is a lifetime commitment. Once they are off to college or out of the home, they are young adults. They are released into this world. Just as your Father in Heaven will never leave you, as a parent you must never leave your children. I'm not telling you to carry their burdens. Teach them that God is their source. He can solve any problem. They must build their relationship with our Father. They need your prayers, they need advice, and they need encouragement. Show them how to stay positive in negative situations. These are things you teach them. It teaches them faith. If they are rebellious, pray in silence from afar. Some need a lesson a few times before they get it. Every lesson that comes brings them a blessing. When they look back, it's a testimony. Reflecting later, they will know their parents were there for them, giving them ideas and new ways to look at things. You are teaching them how to renew their mind in all things. No matter what is being said or done at any given moment, things can change. Don't give up. Your negative will change to a positive. Where is your faith? Now faith is given by the Lord (see Hebrews 11:1-6). Pass on everything you know to your seeds. It's a beautiful sight to see each generation get stronger and stronger. God always has a plan for our future (see Jeremiah 29:11). Be the mother that your children will rise up and call you blessed (see Proverbs 31:28-31).

Dear Father, please protect this madam's children. Keep them healthy and safe. Keep Satan, his demons, and anyone trying to harm them away. Help them to always know that they are loved and protected. Help them to make good choices. I ask for your precious blood to protect them. Your Holy Spirit cleanses them. Guard them against diseases of mind and body, accidents, predators, and all

kinds of evil and evildoers. In Jesus' name. Amen.
(see Psalm 5:11-12)

If you're not a biological mother, this doesn't mean
that you will not have a nurturing spirit. You don't
need a biological child to take part in this life. A child
is always in need for assorted reasons. Biological is
just blood. Blood doesn't make you family. Your heart
does. Your actions are proof of where your heart is.
What do you demonstrate to a child? Is it love? Is it
protection? Is it peace? Is it a haven? These are the
things that make you a mother. Some adopt children
in need of a mother or parents. Some are godmothers,
spiritual moms, role models, stepmoms, foster moms,
big sisters, etc. Whatever you are called to do, do it
big and bold, and put your name on it. If it's a spiritual
mom, be the best one. Everyone has a place, and it is
up to you to find it. It takes a special woman to build
without the bloodline. You don't have to, but God
knew that you would. You will have a greater appreciation for a multitude of things. A mother comes in many
ways. It's children that need you. Don't be afraid to get

in where you fit in. I love my nieces and nephews like they are my own. There's nothing I wouldn't do for them. I pray for them like they are my own children. It's no different to me. They have a good established mother already, but if she wasn't available, I would still be the same but more. Children, teenagers, and young adults always need a woman's touch.

As a mother, you will need to be connected in the spirit. There are so many gifts just in that alone. Be thankful for all of the love given. I have a few women that love me like a daughter. They have taught me so much in my journey. The love is beyond real. I know our Father in Heaven made this happen. God made this happen for me as a mother, to continue to grow. Guess who benefits from it? The blessed seeds that He trusted me with. I love the sons God blessed me with. It's funny because I had each of them in a different decade: 1995, 2007, and 2013. I have an adult child, a teenager, and an elementary child. God has a sense of humor. That's twelve and six years apart, leaving my oldest and youngest eighteen years apart. My oldest helped me so much with the youngest that the youngest thought he was his dad. Those two favor me so much. They took the Miller side, from my grandfather and his legacy. My middle son is more of my husband's side. My middle son's grandad is Sr. and his dad is Jr. This makes my son *the third*. Let's say he got it honestly. Three generations of strength. I'm beyond grateful!

Being a fivefold madam goes with what feels right. Life isn't perfect, but we make it work. Having agape love for God's people is powerful. We should build God's Kingdom in this manner. God's desire is for us to love our neighbor (see Matthew 22:37-39). A wise woman says to live your life as your eulogy, with no worries about anyone ever having to write it. Have a watchful eye concerning your children. This will protect them from so much. Having a watchful eye changes the world. Use the spiritual eyes He has given you. Spend time in prayer. He will reveal all you need to know. I pray that you will have discernment on how to raise them as children and how to help them as young adult children. Always stay attentive concerning your children. Stay fruitful and in the graces of God. Children need a mother and a father to grow healthy fruit on their tree. Pray for wisdom and strength. Do your part as their mother. Children need to know that they can trust you. If they can trust you, you have changed their lives. They will talk to you. They will communicate freely with you. I pray that your lines of communication are open with your children. They will communicate good and not-so-good feelings. This makes it easy to figure out behavioral problems. Children deal with mental illnesses, bullying, abuse, neglect, etc. You as a mother figure have to have a watchful eye. Keep the lines open for your child to communicate and feel comfortable with you. We can prevent things from happening. We can save our children's lives. We can stop the spread of these things. We don't want underlying damage.

A prayer of a mother avails much. Make time to take your children out on a date. You need one-on-one time with each individual child. My middle son gets out of school on Fridays at 1:30. This is my opportunity to take him to lunch. We talk about school, plans for his future, what college he would like to attend, etc. I have learned to listen to him, and as a result, I'm able to give him better advice. He has received it because I put life on pause for him. At this moment, he knows I care. Children need to know you really care. They need to know that you will fight for them. They need to know there is nothing you will not do for them. This brings security and stability to their lives. Time together changes everything.

No matter the enemy's plans, tell him he can't have your seed. You are called by God. We have the power to create our world. See what God sees in them. Support their dreams. Make sure they are dreaming. Everyone has a life for a reason and purpose. It's up to us to figure it out. What you put out in the universe is up to you. We all need to contribute to the world. My oldest son came really easy for me. I didn't have to try. He was a very special gift to me in my teenage years. I was a baby having a baby. God allowed it because He knew the outcome. This grew me up quickly. I looked at life differently. I graduated high school. I had a job as well while still in high school. My grades in school got better. I made sure to make the honor roll. I was more determined. I started to make plans for our future. My oldest son's siblings didn't come until years and years later. I had fertility issues. The fertility pills didn't work. My husband and I were married for nine years before we conceived our next child. I was devastated and depressed. It was eight years of trying on my own, then with the help of doctors, and it never happened. After the eighth year, my pastor at the time gave me a scripture to stand on. I faithfully prayed that scripture. During this, my pastor came to me to say I was in fear. Fear is the opposite of faith. My husband found a book on faith by Bill Winston in a car he bought right after my pastor told me that. The trunk hadn't been cleaned out, and the book was just sitting there. It was all beat up on the outside of the cover, but the words on the inside were so anointed. The more I read, the bigger my faith got. Sometimes you can have a little faith in things. Sometimes you are called to have crazy big faith. This book helped me to let go of the fear of not getting pregnant for eight years. Not having the miracle I was waiting on had traumatized me. I couldn't see the other side of this gigantic mountain. It was a stronghold that was knocked down by the power of God. He removes the mountains! Whatever it is that is stopping or blocking you, ask the Lord to cast the mountain into the sea (see Matthew 17:20). By faith it's yours. That beat-up book changed our lives. I wrote my daily prayer in my journal. I prayed the same prayer every day. I read the same scripture every day. I stood on it. Because I believed it, nine months later, I conceived a child! Praise you, God. Hallelujah, Jesus.

In that eighth year, I had my new beginning. Something different happened. I read a book and prayed with authority. I did something I never did before to get different results. That last year made it nine years. Our middle son was our miracle seed. I had endometriosis, making it difficult to have children. My God is a healer! It's power in prayer. Who can be against us if God is for us? Use the same power in prayer to cover your children and protect them. Our youngest son came six years later. We weren't even trying. He came so naturally. He was a happy surprise. We weren't even looking. Praise your name, Jesus, for completing it with our children.

As long as I am breathing, I will fight for my children, no matter their age, and you should do the same. Think and speak happy thoughts over their life. Be a praying madam. Be the powerful, loving, kind mother He called you to be. God has a covenant with you. As long as you are breathing, fight in prayer for your children, adult children, grandchildren, godchildren, etc. This is a great requirement for being a warrior-praying mother madam. I pray that you will be the powerful, loving, kind mother God created and called you to be. Stand firm and tall on what you believe. God will surely protect your children as long as they live. God will honor the covenant he has with you. Fast, pray, believe, and it is so.

Lord, give this warrior mom wisdom, discernment, understanding, favor, love, compassion, peace, joy, and strength to be an on-time mother madam. Break every generational curse that the enemy tried to put on their children. Satan, we bind you in the name of Jesus! You can't have our seeds. I command you to let go now in the name of Jesus Christ! Let go and loose them! You have no power! You are powerless. Get your hands off! You are blocked and cut off at the roof. We renounce you, Satan! We rebuke you in every area of our children's lives. I decree and declare our children to be anointed and blessed from head to toe. These children are complete in you, God. Please put a hedge around her adult children. Let them desire a relationship with you. Let them learn how to build a relationship with you, the Father. I love you, Lord! Amen!

Release your children in God's secure hands. He will protect them from all harm. I pray that your children will always feel loved and accepted. Ask God to be the head of your children. It's so important for them to have and establish their own relationship with their Father in Heaven. This starts as a child. They practice what they see. My middle son, at the age of one, could barely talk, but he was singing, "Yes, Jesus Loves Me." Why? Because for the first year of his life, I sang that song to him every day. One day, he unexpectedly started singing along with me. Quality time with your children teaches them how to be in a relationship and how to love and value a relationship. Make sure they carry this with them. This can happen from generation to generation. Teach them how to have a loving relationship with their siblings. The first family is the most important relationship. It can follow you into adulthood. Make it right with your first family. When you go into your second family, you don't want to bring baggage. Behavior patterns and problems need to be worked out. Having your first family healthy enhances self-esteem and healthier behaviors. Families are different, and some break. The God I serve will put those broken pieces back together. It can be better than before. It's called restoration. If He did it for my family, He most certainly can do it for yours. Conflict will come. How will we deal with it? Putting on the armor of God and fighting is the best way. Protect your children. Communicate with them. Always keep your word to children. This builds their confidence and trust in you. My grandmother, Carrie Miller, stood on this word. She knew Psalm 23 by heart, and so did we. If you were around her, you were going to know it too.

Together, we can be a dedicated team. As a parent, your job is to teach, discipline, and provide for your children. There is so much to teach and train. There are different seasons and levels in life. As we go through this, we are learning and growing all in one. It takes longer than eighteen years. You should see the fruit of what you are teaching them in their daily lives. You should see it on their report cards, in their behavior, when they're playing sports, in their attitudes, etc. The big foundation should be God. At two years old, my miracle seed son's first vocabulary was all about Jesus. The church and everyone were so blessed by him. He gave them hope. What was demonstrated was so rare to see. Training and love are the keys to a happy child. It carries them a long way in life. I stopped working for two years. I stayed at home and poured into my son. I knew who God said he was. I kept his face covered and didn't bring him out. It was at least four to six months before anyone saw him outside of the immediate family. Treasure your children; they are precious. If you don't, who will? My oldest had a tough time getting up in the mornings. I would yell his name: "Jut, Jut, Jut." The middle son was just a baby at the time. By the time he was six months old, he started yelling out too: "Jut!" My husband and I couldn't believe it. It was so hilarious. Kids are watching everything you do, good or bad. They are like sponges, soaking up everything. Speak good and teach them good. This baby was doing supernatural things early.

Let's talk about discipline. Spare the rod and spoil the child (see Proverbs 13:24). If you don't correct them when they are wrong, they will go the wrong way. They want to know what is right. Loving them is a part of correcting them. Every child is different. Find out how you should discipline them. What works for one child might not work for the other. My best advice is to call on Jesus for guidance. Learn about your child and how to handle them in discipline. "Pour out your heart like water in the presence of the Lord. Lift up your hands to him for the lives of your children" (Lamentations 2:19).

God has a plan (see Jeremiah 29:11). Having kids is a sacrifice. Put them first and make sure they have what they need. They don't stay young forever. One day, the role will change. They will take care of you. The seeds you have sown will come back. This is a blessing to see. Anyone can start off being family by blood. Your heart is what makes you family. It doesn't always come by blood.

A child's job is to cooperate and respect their parents (see Exodus 20:12). Having a godly foundation from the start means that when they stray, they will eventually return. I'm the first to raise my hand on this one. I grew up with that foundation, and as an adult, I made some choices. I didn't always make the best decision for me, but as I got older and made many mistakes, I learned from my past experiences. If it wasn't for my foundation, I would have been lost. That most definitely saved me.

Let's talk about education. Education is the most powerful weapon that you can use to change the world. Our children are our future. The world is waiting. School is their goal to succeed. If they struggle, get help. Find a tutor that fits your child. Ask for your child to stay after for extra help. Do what's necessary to get them working independently. My oldest had homework at three years old. We did a sheet every evening. He was guaranteed to be an honor roll student. He truly was an honor student, as were his younger brothers. Sit with them early on to help them build confidence.

Teachers play a role, but parents play the biggest role. It's not the teacher's job to instruct your child alone. Parents, put your hands in it. Watch them grow. It's a two-part process. Do not forget that academics come before sports. If your grades are not in order, you're not ready for other activities. College can be challenging. They may not be ready to be sent off for four years of school. That should be okay too. However, your child does need some kind of education. It could be a trade school. It could be a community college to get a degree. Find the fit for your child. What do they want to be? What does it require?

Set rules in your house. Create daily chores when they are little, and add more as they get older. This sets them up for success. Create clean habits for the rest of their life. A clean home creates a healthy environment. It brings order, peace, and comfort in your life. If you are winning in life, you can count on order being there. This builds structure and character. This is also true for your appearance and being groomed well. These things need to be taught and practiced in order to bring perfection. Your finances flow better when your house is in order and clean. Positive energy flows and this eliminates stress. You can attract wealth by your thoughts and thinking. I must admit that training boys in household duties has been a big challenge for my husband and me. It's worse than potty training. This too shall pass. It's not our favorite thing to train on. It's like repeatedly beating a drum.

Your children are what makes you a family (see Proverbs 22:6). The family that prays together stays together. My grandmother had this scripture all through her house, with praying hands on a sculpture. I watched her go to her bed in the middle of the day. After she cooked, she would go pray. I learned so much from her daily routine. I was very observant early on. Her prayers helped and blessed so many. She demonstrated that family means having someone to love you unconditionally despite your shortcomings. Family helps us get through the most challenging times. We all need each other in different seasons. Madams, make prayer your beginning, and the strength of it changes everything.

Questions to ask yourself: What do I need to pray for concerning my children? What area can I approve of in my children's life to make it better? God always shows you what's important concerning your children. Listen to what you hear. Also, watch what you see.

Let us pray.

Dear Lord, I pray for this madam as she looks for you to be her strength and guidance concerning her children. Grant her the gift of wisdom on how to bless her children. I pray for her family to always stay together. Have her children rise up and call her blessed. She has pure love for her family. She is a Proverbs 31 woman. Let her always lead by the best example, carrying the Holy Spirit within her. I pray for her young children and adult children to have a solid foundation in you. As their seeds and families grow, keep your hand upon them, so that generation to generation will pour into one another in abundance. I decree and declare for your children to increase in wisdom and prosperity in all areas of their life. Your children's children are blessed. Amen.

CHAPTER 4

THE MINISTRY

Your ring finger represents your ministry. It is a symbol of eternal love, beauty, creativity, power, stability, responsibility, and balance.

Women in the ministry is a beautiful blessing. The anointing follows you, madam. We are offered an opportunity to study God's word, serve others, and give to others. Simply, we are women connecting with women and encouraging their walk in Christ. This can come in many different forms. As a child, I served in the church as a singer, usher, girl scout, and Sunday school student. I loved serving and helping. Singing brought me so much joy. As an adult, I served as a praise dancer. The anointing falling upon me in dancing was a sure blessing from God. From this, God's people were blessed to receive. This was my most cherished gift that He gave me in ministry. It was the most heartfelt and sincere gift that I have received. How beautiful are the feet of those who preach the gospel. I watched my mom serve as a leader on the usher board committee. That was her act of service, which she loved. She loved taking care of God's people. My grandmother sang on the choir as a soprano. She was the head of the pastor's aide. She did the welcome when visitors came. Her beautiful smiling face was the first one people saw, and she was quite the fashionista. They knew who to put at the front to welcome visitors. Her presence made everyone smile and feel welcomed. All these are gifts that we use for His Kingdom. God will put His power on your natural strength. I have been in a couple of women's ministries, where women came together in a small setting, learning and studying God's word. When we come together with different gifts and talents, we create a beautiful body of Christ (see 1 Corinthians 12:12). Ministry takes place within the body. How is the ministry being set apart and different? It's simply serving and offering up spiritual sacrifices pleasing to God.

There are five functions of ministry: worship, teaching, fellowship, evangelism, and serving. I love to worship as an adult. As a child, I loved to serve. Everyone can partake in these gifts. We all have one. It's up to you to find your gift. Here are some ideas on how to find your gift inside of you:

1. Ask God what His will is for you.

2. Find your passions.

3. Take a spiritual gift test.

4. Visit different ministries before you commit.

5. Push past your comfort zone.

6. Pray for revelation.

Father God, please help this madam to find her gift. Let her use it well. I pray that you anoint her in what you have predestined and called her to do. Also, if she has gifts that she hasn't discovered yet, please show her what's next. Let her have hunger, fire, and desire to use her gifts. Let her be confident and strong. Cover this madam in the blood of Jesus. When she hears your voice, I pray for revelation and understanding. She will move in the Spirit. In the name of Jesus. Amen.

You

I confess that I am a madam. I will find my gifts in the ministry. I will use them for the Kingdom. I will do what's pleasing to you, Father. I decree and declare that I carry a Christ-like character all the days of my life. Amen.

After seeking God, He will reveal your gifts through the Holy Spirit. As you unfold what your gift is, ask God to teach you and show you how. He will develop you into your gift. It takes spending time with God, reading the Word, and studying the Word. Start exercising your gift. This brings spiritual maturity. Use your gifts to serve others for the benefit of the body. This is all for the glory of God. Each believer is given at least one gift. Don't stop there. The Holy Spirit decides who receives which gifts. I want to share a few gifts that the Lord has given to the church.

Pastor/Shepherd - Caring for the personal needs of others by nurturing and mending life issues, and teaching from the Bible to those within the congregation (see 2 Timothy 4:2).

Leadership - Motivating people to work together in unity toward common goals (see Romans 12:8).

Administration - Making sure others stay on task and stay organized (see 1 Corinthians 12:28).

Teaching - Instructing members in the truths and doctrines of God's word, and building up and maturing the body (see Ephesians 4:11).

Knowledge - Teaching and training people to learn and know and explain the precious truths of God's word with a spirit that reveals truth (see 1 Corinthians 12:28).

Wisdom - Discerning the work of the Holy Spirit in the body, understanding, and bringing clarity (see 1 Corinthians 12:28).

Prophecy - Proclaiming the Word of God boldly and communicating God's truth and heart in a way that calls people to a right relationship with God. By building up the body, prophecy manifests itself through preaching and teaching (see Romans 12:6).

Discernment - Spiritually identifying falsehoods through divine strength and distinguishing between right and wrong motives and spiritual forces at work. Being able to grasp and understand what is obscure and hard to see (see 1 Corinthians 12:10).

Intercession - Standing in the gap in prayer for someone or something and believing in profound results (see Ephesians 6:18).

Exhortation - Good counseling, motivating others thoroughly, and encouraging people (see Romans 12:8).

Tongues - Praying in heavenly language to encourage your spirit and to commune with God. This gift can be accompanied by interpretation (see 1 Corinthians 14:27-28).

Faith - Believing in God and for unseen supernatural results in every area of life (see Hebrews 11:1).

Apostleship – Having divine strength to pioneer new churches through planting, overseeing, and training (see Ephesians 2:20).

Evangelism - Helping non-Christians take necessary steps to become a born-again Christian (see Matthew 28:19-20).

Giving - Producing wealth and giving tithes and offerings for the purpose of advancing the Kingdom of God on earth (see Proverbs 3:19-10).

Healing - Intermediating in faith and prayer by laying on of hands for healing physical, mental, and spiritual sickness (see James 5:14-15).

Hospitality - Creating a warm and welcoming environment for others in places such as your home and church (see 1 Timothy 5:10).

Miracles - Positioning oneself to receive miracles through repentance and forgiveness by meditating on God's word and asking, listening, and expecting God to have divine direction. Faith comes as we hear from God (see Acts 3:2-8 and Matthew 21:21).

Let's talk about the Holy Spirit.

Who is the Holy Spirit?

The Holy Spirit is the third person of the Trinity, co-equal and co-eternal with the Father and the Son. The Bible says that the Holy Spirit is a person, not a force of power, and He possesses all the attributes of God. He is the source of spiritual life, power, and gifts, and works to carry out God's purpose in the world. Jesus promised to send the Holy Spirit to be with His disciples and to dwell in them after his departure. The Holy Spirit is described as the helper, who will guide them into all truth and comfort them in their troubles (see John 14:16-17).

The Holy Spirit is mentioned in the Old and New Testament. In the Old Testament, the Holy Spirit is described as the Spirit of God, the Spirit of the Lord, and the Spirit of wisdom and understanding. In the New Testament, the Holy Spirit is often referred to as the comforter, counselor, and helper, and is associated with the indwelling of believers, spiritual gifts, and sanctification (see Romans 8:9-11).

1. It is important to invite the Holy Spirit in every day of your life. Do this through prayer and meditation on the Word of God. Ask Him to reveal Himself to you and guide you daily (see John 14:16-17).

2. Be open to be led by the Holy Spirit. Listen to His voice and obey His promptings (see Romans 8:9-11).

3. Cultivate the fruit of the Holy Spirit in your life. When walking in the Spirit, you will produce love, joy, peace, patience, kindness, goodness, faithfulness, gentleness, and self-control (see Galatians 5:22-23).

As you seek Him with a humble and open heart, He will reveal Himself to you in ways that will transform you. May the Holy Spirit empower you to live a life that brings honor and glory to God. May it bring so many blessings to you.

Let us pray!

Lord, bring a balance to this madam. Let her invite your Holy Spirit to live in her, and let your Spirit be her teacher, comforter, and best friend. Holy Spirit, reveal yourself. Please be her daily guide. Let her listen to your guidance and direction. Let her discern the thoughts that you give her. She builds a relationship and knows it's you, Lord. The Holy Spirit develops character in her. She is a madam of excellent quality. Lead and guide her in all truth. This fivefold madam bears healthy fruit that glorifies God. In the mighty name of Jesus Christ. Amen!

God gave us His Son as a gift. Today, the Son of God is seated at the right hand of God. Jesus is in the realm of eternal glory (see Ephesians 1:20), and He gave us the Holy Spirit. He is the comforter that will teach you all things. The Holy Spirit brings all things to our remembrance

(see John 14:25-27). The Holy Spirit is your guide in choosing. He is the part in your mind that always speaks for the right choice. The Holy Spirit is the way in which God's will is done on earth as it is in Heaven. God gives gifts to his people to manifest the Holy Spirit and to build up one another in faith. Spiritual gifts help build love and unity in the church as each person uses what they received for the good of one another.

There are seven characteristics of the Holy Spirit: wisdom, understanding, counsel, fortitude, knowledge, piety, and fear of the Lord. He is known as the comforter. He can calm our fears and fill us with hope. He can guide us in our decisions and protect us from physical and spiritual danger. Through His power, we are sanctified as we repent, receive saving ordinance, and keep our covenants. The Holy Spirit will often speak to us in our minds by giving us a thought or an idea. Oh, how I love the Holy Spirit, my best friend and teacher. Praise you, God!

The Holy Spirit will lead us by making impressions upon our hearts. By saying something, doing something, or thinking something according to God's will, we are being led by the Spirit of God. The presence of God is a part of a person's religious experience. The feeling of having the Holy Spirit can be gratitude, peace, reverence, love, or burning in the bosom.

There are three steps to receiving the Holy Spirit. First, have faith in our Heavenly Father and His beloved Son, Jesus Christ. Second, be clean. Third, have pure motives. Want them for the right reasons. Then the Holy Spirit will be beside us, within us, upon us, and filling us.

Praise and Worship

Music in worship helps us to learn about God. Hymns and choirs are all a part of worship. Dance is a means to express worship, thanks, or adoration to God, or to tell a story. This is all a part of praise and worship. We have musical instruments as well. All these are used to glorify our God. Music designed by God moves both spirit and mind (see Corinthians 14:15). Music brings spiritual awakening. It brings out strong emotions. It brings unity in a spiritual connection. Sing to God! Sing praises to him. Tell of all his wonderful acts (see Psalm 105:2). Praise him with tambourine and dance. David danced before the Lord with all his might. He showed a terrific example of what it truly means to surrender to God in worship (see 2 Samuel 6:14-22). Dancing unto God is sacred. Dancing is excellent for communicating, connecting, or expressing emotions. God loves to hear you sing, even if you think your voice isn't that good.

Come, let us sing for joy to the Lord; let us shout aloud to the Rock of our salvation. Let us come before him with thanksgiving and extol him with music and song. Music, singing, dancing, and instruments have the power to lift you up. These are all beautiful ways to express our love to God. Worshipping through music changes and transforms us. "Create in me a pure heart, O God" (Psalm 51:10).

I'm so glad that God gave us all distinct gifts. We are to find these gifts and exalt them. Build them up for His Kingdom. It brings glory to our Father in Heaven. We are the body of Christ. Let's make it beautiful. Amen!

CHAPTER 5

BUSINESS

Your pinky finger represents your business, meaning your intelligence and intuition.

Being a businesswoman is a sure determination that you are becoming a fivefold woman. The Bible clearly says that a Proverbs 31 woman (verses 10-31) is an ideal entrepreneur. She is industrious, generous, and pious in all her actions. She is godly, devoted, respected, noble, and full of wisdom. She makes linen garments and sells them, and supplies the merchants with sashes. She sees that her trading is profitable and good. She selects wool and flax and works with eager hands. She is like the merchant ships, bringing her food from afar. She gets up while it is still night, and she provides food for her family and portions for her female servants. She considers a field and buys it; out of her earnings, she plants a vineyard. Her lamp does not go out at night. She watches over the affairs of her household and does not eat bread of idleness (see Proverbs 31:16-17).

The good news is that if a woman sets her mind on something, she will get it done no matter what. Shout because you are a phenomenal woman. God created us to be great women through His might and strength. There is nothing that we can't do without Him. Our special powers here on earth are in Christ Jesus. His anointing removes burdens and destroys yokes of bondage. Praise Him right now for His greatness. Our anointing is believing and receiving His word. It's the truth and the way of life.

As followers of Jesus, He has given us all that we will ever need. His blood is our forever-lasting protection. Seal yourself in it daily. You are made to be a woman of power. Own this and walk in it. Anything outside of that is not for you.

God created men and women equal in value, yet unique in form and function. Your form and function consist of you being a precious daughter, wife, hard worker, homemaker, businesswoman, teacher, and friend. You can sum this up to being a fivefold madam of the Lord. She gives to the poor and has children who bless her, with able means to have the power or skill to do so. Madam, you are able. Count your blessings.

Madam, you can create your own world and environment. You can pick what career you want. You have a choice in the matter of your life. Sometimes it doesn't go as planned. Never give up! Believe what you say. Put some action to it. It's okay to reset the button. What you choose and believe is for you. Have big faith in a world where your Lord has given you power. "I have given you authority to trample on snakes and scorpions and to overcome all the power of the enemy; nothing will harm you" (Luke 10:19).

When you hear the word *behold,* there is power behind it. *Behold* means to stop at once and look intensely. He said He gives unto us *power!* God is giving us special, supernatural protection against these natural dangers. God has given us authority over all the power of the devil. Know who you are. You must speak this. You must believe this. You must confess this. Use the power He has given to you against the devil. You are a winner. God has called you *victorious!* Sometimes you must fight for it. Exercise your faith daily. The word is the truth. God will never break His promise. He is a promise keeper. God is creator and Lord over everything.

Let's consider the word *able*, which means we have the ability to solve a problem, having freedom or opportunity to do something—to simply have power! Some of you have had great women come before you, a great line of women who set a fine example. Some of you will have to be that example for your legacy. That's okay too, because you either carry the cycle or create one. God has your spirit because of what you missed in the past. Move forward in your present and future. I guarantee you your sister has it. I guarantee you your spiritual mom has it. I guarantee you your aunt has it. I guarantee you that someone in your life will have it. Automatically you will have it. Through various times and seasons, God knows when you're ready for a new level. No one knows all of this at once. We grow and we go through life in many different ways and seasons. Make sure you are growing through and learning from each chapter. You can't do it all. You need to rely on His strength and wisdom. God knows who you need in your life. He will send them at the right time. Some people are in your life for a blessing. Some are for a lesson. Keep God first in everything that you do. He is your Heavenly Father. He loves you more than you love yourself. He is your creator. You are amazingly beautiful.

The Hebrew word for God Almighty is El Shaddai (see Genesis 17:1-2). He is the God who is more than enough, more than sufficient. This means that He has the power to complete promises of blessings and prosperity. Hallelujah! Thank you, Lord Jesus Christ. God can show you (see Romans 16:25). When you were born, you knew nothing, but God was able to make all grace abound toward you (see 2 Corinthians 9:8). It's His grace that keeps us in all of our ways. God has watched you grow through so many stages in your life, from a baby to a toddler and on through being a teenager, young adult, adult, parent, and grandparent. You have had good fruit and some not-so-good fruit. We are blessed that He can remove mountains from your life. God wants you to bear good healthy fruits. I choose to line up to His word.

Spiritual Pruning

God wants to prune you. Pruning means to preserve something, to cut off or cut back parts for a better shape or a more fruitful growth. This is a reward from God to you. Praise Him! Spiritual pruning enhances spiritual growth. This happens by removing whatever inhibits spiritual growth. Let God be your vinedresser. He wants you to bear the fruit of Christ (be(you)tiful). The more pruned, the more fruits. Those dead branches must go (see John 15). God wants us as born-again believers to progress from barrenness to fruitfulness to spiritual abundance. He is the vine and we are the branches. Stay connected to the source. Your cell phone has a source. You wouldn't dare disconnect from that source. You find ways to connect whether outside of your home, in your car, or elsewhere. Some even have a cordless charger so the battery is always charged. You stay ready, and it's the same with the original source. Stay connected and invested. Stay plugged into the real plug that is the Lord Jesus Christ.

With God continuously showing up in your life, He is surely creating you to be the powerful woman that we love to see. Madam, you are not an overnight process. You're like the slow cooker in your kitchen, which is the best way to prepare your food. Meanwhile, there are relationships that you really love, the ones you simply can't live without. If it's not healthy for you, you have to let it go. Ask yourself, does this relationship drain me? How does this person make me feel? Are you always on edge? God will show you and confirm to you the individual who's blocking your blessings just by being in your life. All the good things that God pours into you are being sucked out by the individuals who are holding you back. Be careful and aware of the wrong animal spirit in your life. It is a seductive spirit that roams, an anaconda rattlesnake spirit that is looking to devour you. Its poisonous venom will try and destroy your life.

I'm speaking from personal experience. I have to be real with what I have been through. I know this will help someone. Tell the truth and shame the devil! The anaconda spirit came upon me. I prayed and called a few friends to help me pray. It worked at first, but the spirit came back months later. This time things changed. My marriage took a turn for the worse. I was hurt, confused, angry, and off balance. When the spirit came back, it was different. I was different and not my usual self. There were some hurtful truths regarding infidelity in my marriage. I didn't want to work it out. I didn't want marriage counseling. My feelings and emotions were damaged. The enemy used this to attack. I was a baptized and saved woman of God, but my guard was let down.

The enemy looks for ways to come in and destroy you. He will use any cracked window or open door. Be careful who you call a sister, brother, friend, and lover. Be careful and mindful of the people you let in your life. The enemy comes in all forms, and he comes when you're most vulnerable and when you're not looking. He wants you to be off guard. He roams around looking for a way in. I inherited an able spirit. I come from the blood lineage of my grandmother. She was a praying woman, and she had already groomed me. Physically I can't swim, but mentally and spiritually I can swim. Once that anaconda spirit grabbed me, I was in the deep water. Mentally and spiritually, I had to fight with the word. I had to fight with everything that had been spiritually deposited in me to save my life. To come out of that water, that spirit had to release me from the deep. When it spit me out, it felt like I landed in a jungle. All the pain and hurt put me into a place where I gave up. I was most definitely bit in the spirit. It changed my life. My family was broken. We were all damaged by this, but all three of my children loved me unconditionally. They were there right by my side, and now I know why He blessed me with three sons. Spiritually I was broken. This virtuous Proverbs 31 woman was broken. But they stood by my side just like the Lion of Judah. They demonstrated such strength and courage. During that time, they were also hurting, as their life had been changed as well, but they never left my side.

The dark pit I was in caused depression, but God never took His righteous hands off me. I experienced life, and it made me the strongest I have ever been. Pain builds character and strength. God delivered me and my family from the enemy's hand. When experiencing pain, there is a choice that needs to be made. My choice was to finally let go and let God work. I began to pray harder than ever. My prayer language and communication with God got stronger. My entire family learned a valuable lesson through this season. You know the saying, "What doesn't kill you will make you stronger." This was a three-year season that we went through, and trust me, my God was working the entire time. God allowed us to be stripped all the way down, but He already knew He would build us up. To be honest, we didn't know that. We thought our family had come to an end. We thought it was over. But everything had to crash so we could be rebuilt.

The way God came shocked us. All I can say after all of that is, "But God. Hallelujah!" The foundation this time was solid ground. We were building bricks! I began to release all the poison out of my belly. Six months later, I gave my marriage a chance again, but only after releasing things that were draining me. My husband also had to let go of things in his life. He had to release that same venom poison out of his belly. We were driving together one day, and he said that he felt nauseous and dizzy. I had already been through this and immediately knew what it was. I told him to pull over. He pulled over immediately. I told him to cough, and he began to cough over and over. It came up and out. I told him that more should come out. He coughed some more, and it came up and out again. I told him to try it some more, and even this third time, it came up and out again. The number three represents the Father, Son, and Holy Spirit. He was in disbelief at what happened, and I was praising God.

When yokes come up, deliverance comes. The seeds of the enemy can no longer control you. I praise God for the healing and deliverance that took place in each of us. I confess we haven't been the same since then. I knew at that moment that we could start again. God's work was complete. He had favored our family. This is our testimony: no matter what it looks like and no matter how bad it gets, God our Father in Heaven has all power in His hands. He can restore any situation at any time. If some situations in your life are dead, God can resurrect them. He brought Jesus back from the dead, so your situation is nothing for Him to bring back to life. He is the greatest problem solver you will know. He is the undefeated King of kings, the Lord of lords, the mighty and magnificent one.

My best and favorite thing God did for me is PTR. This means to *Protect*, *Transform*, and *Restore*. There are no patch-ups in the Kingdom. There is only complete transformation. The old houses that get reconstructed—the new way to say it is *gutted out*—those are the best kind of houses. They are sturdy, durable, solid, and specially crafted and designed. A solid foundation! This is all part of the pruning process or stage, and it's not a pretty sight.

Things can get attached to you if you allow them to. I'm here to tell you that if anyone or anybody is sucking the air out of you, let them go in the name of Jesus! Let go of everything that is dead or holding you back. Let God prune you. Some relationships will have you in a spiritual place where you have no business. Have the right people in your life. Don't be led by the wrong voice. Don't let a person come into your life that comes with spirits attached to them. Watch how they treat and talk to you. Pay attention to both sides of the person. Beware of an open door for evil to come in. Shut that door and lock it. No one has access and control over your life. You are the leader of your life. Don't give anyone this kind of power in your life. You know what's not right. God is your creator. Trust in Him. Ask His Holy Spirit to lead you daily. That's all you need in your daily walk. He is the truth and light. God is ready to prune, remake, transform, and flourish you.

Madam of the Lord, take your peace back. Your spiritual connection with the Father is important. Keep those lines of communication open. God will show you who to bless and when. Your money is yours, period. When family members or friends are wanting to borrow money from you, it is the wrong season to be in. In order to keep your blessing, be good stewards and in the spirit. Let no one lead you astray.

After all the storms I went through, in the end, God upgraded me. I started a new teaching career. I didn't see that coming. It had never been my dream to teach, but I must say that I fell in love with those kids right away. I really loved my new career. It was a gift to put me in a classroom to shape and mold children from an educational perspective. It has been truly amazing. I have a natural gift with the kids. I am a licensed cosmetologist as well, and I have been in the industry for twenty years. The kids love to sit in my chair. This showed me to dream more, to do new things, and be creative. God made us to explore the world and to try different and challenging things. This brings you out of your comfort zone, but it is well worth the reward. My purpose involves the lives of many children. This changes them forever, resulting in healthy-minded, growing, and thriving children. That's what I love to witness. They grow and learn from year to year. It's an honor to witness this. Not to brag, but kids really love me. The light God has put on me brings them love and joy. It's an amazing experience and a blessing and honor to be in their life. These kids are the future. I'm glad to have a hand in education. If I can help create a solid foundation for these kids, I will choose that every time. The love I have for them is unapologetic. Thank you, Lord, for this blessing and gift.

My family has been through a lot, but look at the picture God painted for me. I get to live it out loud. Don't believe the negativity or the picture the enemy has painted. God has *all power!* The weapons may form but the weapons will not prosper. Praise Him in the midst of your storm. I was in a place where I couldn't see my way through. Three years later, my husband and I were standing at the end of that road. The road split, and he went one way and I went another. At the end, we looked at each other and both agreed that travelling the road separately was hell. We both learned valuable lessons. It changed us at our very core.

God was pruning and changing us all along. It was a process to go through to get what we have now. All the pain and hurt was necessary. It made us stronger than before. We were able to overcome and heal. We connected on a really deep level mentally, spiritually, physically, emotionally, and sexually. We have not been the same. God turned an old situation into a new one. Deliverance took place in our marriage and family. The power of God moved into our house. We decided to keep our house and remodel it. It meant a lot to see our old house become a new healthy home. It became up-to-date, and every room had brand-new furniture and decorations. We even got a brand-new kitchen and appliances. It was a complete makeover. God saved us. He saved everything.

As mentioned earlier, there is a saying that women marry the person they admired growing up, such as a father, grandfather, uncle, or close relative. Well, I have to say that my husband is like my grandfather in so many ways that I can hardly believe it. They have the same personality and zodiac sign. I tease him a lot and say, "Why are you acting like daddy?" He doesn't fuss. He just looks at me and says, "Wrong guy." He does not argue with me. My granddaddy was the same lol.

Dear Lord, I want to thank you for delivering me from the enemy's hand. I want to thank you for restoring my life and making my family life better than before. I ask you to deliver this woman of God from the hand of the enemy. Deliver her from any trap that has been set. Break every chain and free her from the curse of the law. Open her eyes and let her see spiritually. Restore her life in every way that's needed. I pray that her health and wealth get better. I pray that she has the strength to cut off everything causing her not to live her best life. Prune this madam. Nothing will stop the life you have planned for this fivefold madam (see Jeremiah 29:11). She is your treasured and favored daughter. In the name of Jesus. Amen.

"Praise the Lord, my soul, and forget not all his benefits—who forgives all your sins and heals all your diseases, who redeems your life from the pit and crowns you with love and compassion, who satisfies your desires with good things so that your youth is renewed like the eagle's" (Psalm 103:2-5).

Jealousy

What does *jealousy* mean? To be jealous is to feel resentment, bitterness, or hostility toward someone because they have something that you don't. This feeling or the state of feeling this way is called jealousy. "This is my commandment, that you love and unselfishly seek the best for one another, just as I have loved you" (John 15:12).

Jealousy. This is a much-needed topic. If you're a human who is not perfect, you have felt the emotion of jealousy. No one is perfect, and at some point, you have felt this emotion. Even babies early on feel this emotion. Siblings more than anything will have the experience of being jealous of one another as they fight for their parents' attention and approval. If this is not handled correctly early on, they could carry this on as adults. It ruins relationships that God meant for good and peace. As a child, I was jealous of my sister from as young as five years old. I can remember not being kind to her simply because I wanted to be the oldest. These were my thoughts as a child. She looked like Penny from *Good Times*, the TV show, so she was very pretty. I didn't care if I was pretty too, I was just looking at it from what she had going on. I couldn't see my own potential. I was just worried about what she had going on. This damaged our relationship early on. It was selfish, and a lot of us still think this way. That's why we need to have a forgiving spirit. If she never forgave me, we wouldn't have a relationship today. We have to forgive if we want to be forgiven when we choose wrong. Everyone chooses wrong sometimes. If you haven't yet, it's just not your turn yet. The key is learning from your mistakes, doing better, and never repeating them.

I didn't know being the oldest requires a lot more energy. You're held to a standard to be the example. It's challenging work if you do it right. I didn't know that she was going to be my best friend. No matter the age, the older we got, the stronger our bond grew. After I graduated high school, it got better and better. She was my protector. I have learned to embrace all of her unique qualities. I learn from her, and she learns from me as well. We are a blessed twosome that God has molded. I guarantee there is some individual jealousy over our friendship being blood sisters. Why do they do everything together? Why do they live in the same neighborhood? How do they prosper together? It's God's mercy and grace working in our life. We are prayer partners and we totally surrender ourselves to the Father. That's why we are blessed to have such a wonderful relationship instead of living with jealousy or judgment. Admire this and ask, "How do y'all do it?" We don't mind sharing with others. We can't take the credit for his abundance in our life. We know why and how. It's having the Lord Jesus Christ in our daily walk.

I can remember back in my school days, and sometimes still now, that beautiful girls would be distant to me. They would look around me and avoid eye contact. I never did anything to them. I never even talked negatively about them. But just because I looked different from them, they would ignore me. Still to this day, if I am out and see some beautiful girls who I know, it's a dry hello. Sometimes they even turn their heads away. I can feel the envious spirit. My life isn't perfect, and I have had to face challenges just like we all have. If we can be honest with ourselves, we need to stop this behavior. It's not becoming. It breaks my heart to see this. We are way past childhood, and we should put away childish things. We have families and people we are responsible for. The love of God should show up when you see a light inside of another woman. Iron sharpens iron. You can admire others, and it doesn't have to be a famous person. Sometimes it's just a local down-to-earth lady. If you see good in a person, be happy about it. We all have different gifts and talents. It's up to you to find them. Your gift will look different from mine, but that doesn't matter. Stop comparing everything. Whose is better? Change your thinking! Cheer for her, because when it's your turn, you will know who didn't clap for you. It's not a good feeling. Rebuke jealousy in the name of Jesus! Amen.

Don't allow a jealous person to affect your confidence or to create self-doubt. Keep doing what you're doing, and don't allow others to stop you. Focus on people who support you. Remind yourself that they're jealous because you are doing something well. Pray for them when it's a close relationship. Ask God to deliver them from this.

Sometimes husbands and wives will have to deal with a jealous spirit. It may be that he is trying to control her because he is insecure. Maybe he is afraid of losing her. He might do things such as check up on her, try to tell her what to do (or not do) and how to act, or limit her contact with friends and coworkers. He could have low self-esteem. Most times jealousy occurs because there is an insecurity and a lack of something in your heart and soul. You are missing something, and therefore you can't be a rewarder for someone else.

Jealousy comes in so many forms. We don't claim it as a part of our covenant. We denounce the spirit of jealousy from our hearts and thoughts. Step up and be a madam. Madams are called to love wholeheartedly. We uplift other women. We support and pour into women. We are our greatest strength and inspiration. Love, love, love, and love! Love drowns out all self-ishness, and it never fails. Be a madam of love and kindness.

Sister Madam, don't let anything stop you from being a great and profound woman. Jesus said in John 15:4, "Remain in me, and I also remain in you. No branch can bear fruit by itself; it must remain in the vine."

Be an independent woman, but don't forget the real part. Be God-dependent! To be God-dependent means you are not independent, empowered, and strong apart from God. If you take God out, that means you are self-reliant. The Bible tells us of stories where people tried to be self-reliant instead of obeying God's commands. They didn't wait for God's promises to manifest, and it backfired. Remain humble, and don't ever lose that humility. Know your source and where your power comes from. Embrace the real truth. You need God's guidance, wisdom, strength, and power. Your worth isn't found in your accomplishments. It is found in God alone. In Christ alone is your worth. A God-dependent woman can do all things through Christ who gives you strength (see Philippians 4:19).

From Sarah to Queen Esther to the Virgin Mary, the Bible is full of women who were dependent on God. A Godly woman never fails to seek God in everything that she does (see 1 Chronicles 16:11).

Madam of God, you are strong, brave, kind, and faithful. You are powerful, anointed, and full of grace. Know who you are. God isn't concerned with outside beauty. He focuses on the inside, your heart and spirit. This is the beauty that God wants from you. A woman who has respect for the Lord should be praised. Proverbs 31:30 says, "Charm is deceptive, and beauty is fleeting, but a woman who fears the Lord is to be praised." What it means is that beauty fades with age, so if you are more concerned with your outer appearance, you will be unhappy when wrinkles come and the number on the scale goes up. Don't get me wrong, personal grooming is important. Look like a queen for your king. But there is a time for everything. He wants to see you beautiful, but your greatest gift to him is a clean and pure heart. Beauty flows from the inside out. We need to be careful of what we put in our bodies, both physically and spiritually. We have a job, and this is why God is our source and power. You are a businesswoman! Go for it!

CONCLUSION

GOD'S HAND!

We are always in His hands, even when we think we don't deserve it. When it's not so obvious or when it is quiet, just know that this is God growing us into what He has called us to be. Let me give you a scripture with evidence that this is true.

Isaiah 41:10 says, "So do not fear, for I am with you; do not be dismayed, for I am your God. I will strengthen you and help you; I will uphold you with my righteous right hand." I don't mind telling my story because I know it was Him. I was in God's hands during it all. No matter how bad my storm got, when I looked to the right and left of me, there was God! Even when there seemed to be no way possible, I came out a winner. God restored my family. The relationship between father and sons was restored. God's power is manifested through Christ Jesus. He promises to never forget His people or to break His covenant. We are forever thankful.

God will make your enemy your footstool. His glorious and strong right hand shatters the enemy (see Exodus 15:6). God will defend you. If He is for you, who can be against you? God wants you to put your situations in His hands. Doing this means to trust His word over your feelings. Trust His word over the doctor's reports. Trust His word in a broken judicial system. Trust Him and His word over all things. In a season of drought in your life, or when at the end of the road, trust Him. Your need doesn't move the hand of God, your faith does. By God's right hand, He will comfort and console us in Christ. Wake up every day and hold his right hand. God is both left-handed and right-handed. The right hand works to make people inwardly holy. The left hand works to make people outwardly good. His hands work in different and opposite ways. All power is in His hands. Isaiah 49:16 says, "Behold I, have engraved you on the palms of my hands; your walls are continually before me." This brings so much peace. Choose to live there. Anything disturbing your peace is too high of a price. The gifts God gives you are eternal peace and happiness. If not, check the sender box. Where did this come from? If it's not a gift from our Father, send it back! God hides us and protects us in His hands. Philippians 4:6-7 says, "Do not be anxious about anything, but in every situation, by prayer and petition, with thanksgiving, present your requests to God. And the peace of God, which transcends all understanding, will guard your hearts and your minds in Christ Jesus."

The God we serve is bigger than any problem we could have. The God we serve has never lost a battle. The God we serve has all power in his hands. With that in mind, Madam, don't you ever give up. Seasons come and go, and after every storm, the sun comes out, and sometimes, depending on the size of it, there is a rainbow. God has a covenant with his children. His word is the truth. How you speak it, believe it, and confess it determines your outcome. God will always fight for you.

Life comes in seasons. Everyone loves spring, as it just feels right. A season of winter in your life might not be so fun. Surround yourself with like-minded people. Make sure you're not the smartest in your group. Grow and learn from people who know more than you. Celebrate because you're not in the same place you were before. Continue to grow and improve yourself in your life. You can't act and look the same your entire life. Don't ever stop growing. Be like a seed that's being watered by the Word of God. What kind of tree will you be? A tree that bears good fruit.

She who lives in Him shall hold strength, beauty, and righteousness. Get good at making good choices. Turn on your spiritual eyes and ears. What is God speaking to you? What is He showing you? Do you believe what you're seeing in the spirit realm? Make sure you are thinking good thoughts. Repent of everything that's not like Him. Ask him to remove it. Resist the devil, and he will flee. Say to Satan, "Get away from me!" Cast those thoughts down.

Finally, hear me loud and clear! When you think like a madam, you no longer put up with abuse. If you're in a relationship and you feel alienated, or if you feel stuck, trapped, and alone, know that this is not from your Father. You need a plan to get out. If you are experiencing physical, mental, or emotional abuse, you need to get out. If your children being mistreated, remember that, as their mother, it's your responsibility to stop this malicious behavior and assignment against your child. This can break your child in so many different ways. As a mother, do not allow your partner to abuse you. Not only is it damaging to you, it is also damaging to your children. From a daughter's point of view, it is showing them that this is okay, that this is what love and affection is. From a son's perspective, it will teach them that it is okay to treat their partner that way.

Additionally, children are sensitive and their feelings get easily hurt. This creates low self-esteem. It can cause children to withdraw from their parents, and a connection can be lost. This opens the doors for other things for your kids to get into, such as early sexual encounters. Children could feel neglected, which can lead to depression.

There are so many curses that can come into your home and affect your mental, physical, and emotional well-being. If the enemy can get to your male partner, your family is in trouble. The male leader is the head. What's on the head flows down. As a mother, make sure it's not curses that flow down. Before the entire house gets infected, get out. I know it's easier said than done. That's where your Heavenly Father comes in. You are His daughter, and He will pick you up in His righteous hands. Call upon Him and He will never leave you or forsake you. He will mend your broken heart. I know you're tied to your partner. Pray for God to untie this soul tie. Ungodly soul ties are made to be broken. You have to want to break this before you create generational curses and generational cycles. Your child will become an adult. They will either repeat the cycle or break it. No one has the power to do this on their own. It will take the hand of God in their life and

His power to transform and resurrect wrong thoughts. Bad decisions and behavior problems are counseled out by God. It's never too late to change areas and to start new again. Some people have practiced making wrong choices for over twenty years and are still stuck in the pattern.

The God I serve will cause something to happen in your life, and you will be faced with what to do. Will you change or stay the same? If that doesn't shake you, I'm not sure what will. Some people may be a little more stubborn than others. The Father always gives you a chance over and over to make the right choices. It's up to you, because He will never force Himself on you. It's all free will, and if you choose Him, God will be your solid ground and foundation. We are not perfect people, but we strive for excellence.

A good man will never ask you to put him before the kids. A good man will put you and the kids first, not ever making it a question of the matter. Everyone's needs will be already met. My husband's birthday comes in the spring, and every year on his birthday, he takes us on a shopping spree. He lets us get clothes and shoes. He makes sure that we are taken care of before him on his day. Once we are taken care of, then he will buy something for himself. That is something to tell the world about. He is the most humble and selfless man in the world. Guess who gets to witness these priceless moments? My sons do, and we are so grateful for my husband and their dad.

If you want your partner and believe there is potential, your job is to get out of the way and let God deal with him. Turn your voice off and give him to the Father. Your partner is likely dealing with generational curses that he didn't ask for, and he doesn't know what to do with it. God's anointing and Holy Spirit can heal him. Every man has good qualities, but when the negative parts of him try to come out, we can't accept it.

On the flip side, some of us women can have a bad attitude. When God blesses you with a good man right away, don't lose him because of your lack of respect. I have seen women who have a lot to learn on how to honor, love, and respect a man. If you ask most men, they will say the number one issue is respect. If this is you, repent and ask God to forgive you and show you how to love him. You may not have seen this example before your eyes, but it's never too late. As an adult, you know right from wrong. Choose what's right and do what's right. You cannot escape the consequence of your actions. Make sure you sow good seeds in everything you do. Every day that you wake up, ask the

Lord to be your shield and ask him to lead and guide you in the mighty name of Jesus Christ!

Let's close out in prayer!

Dear Father, I pray that I wrote exactly what you wanted me to. I thank you for leading and guiding me along the way. You, Holy Spirit, who lives in me, has never left me alone. I'm grateful for the opportunity to share with your children. I decree and declare that someone's life changed. Someone has found Christ. Someone has grown closer to you, Heavenly Father. The woman that read this book grew up in so many ways. As she grows, the crown of your glory will be seen. She lights up and leaves a sparkle wherever she goes. She is a glow-up fivefold woman of the Lord. Father, you are the author of our lives. You have plans to prosper her and make her great. We praise your name because, in the end, you will always correct our story. Thank you, Lord. You are righteous and faithful. We grew through everything that we went through. We count it all joy. Thank you for many new beginnings. I decree and declare that we are made over by Christ Jesus! I cover each madam in the precious blood of Jesus Christ. Come forth, madam! God calls you great and phenomenal. You are worth saving. Never lay down, always arise. You have the victory. He will never allow you to fight the battle alone. Use His mighty power, and fight when necessary. Turn a no into a yes. Turn a negative into a positive. We are world changers. Keep your eyes on Him and He will direct your path. God loves you. And so do I.

You are a fivefold madam! You are five times as great a woman than before. Receive the word, believe the word, speak the word, and it is so! Go out and spread your wings and fly, butterfly. You are no longer a caterpillar. You are beautiful with all of your colors. You are made to spread your love, joy, and happiness all around the world. The very people you encounter are there for a special reason. If they can connect to you, their life has changed, just as your life metaphorically changed. The world needs you to fly, butterfly! So fly high! You are your sister's Christ-keeper!

Amen, Amen, and Amen!

ABOUT THE AUTHOR

Lashone Strickland is called to speak new life into the people of God. She is a great encourager for His people. She shares inspiring prophetic words to help with life lessons. She listens to the voice of God speaking healing and victory over the lives of His people. She understands the importance and power of prayer.

Lashone is a follower of Christ. Having a relationship with the Father in Heaven has changed her life forever. She loves the Lord and his Holy Spirit resides in her. She is a beloved daughter of God.

Giving honor and thanks to God for making all things possible. Forever grateful for her husband and their three sons. Building a legacy of healthy generational to generational blessings for her family.

Visit her online at Lashonestrickland.com

Made in the USA
Columbia, SC
25 October 2024

44684980R00076